# JESUS—the WHOLE story

Ronald Wright

By the same author, published by Regency Press (London & New York) Ltd:

What DID God Say? *(1987)*
HAFED a Prince of Persia *(1988)*

Also published by Revelation Press (London)

HAFED & HERMES *(1989)*
*The Tutor and the boyhood friend of Jesus*

# JESUS

## the *whole* story

Ronald Wright

Revelation Press

1989

Published by Revelation Press, 5 Mead Lane, Hertford SG13 7AG



ISBN 0 9514038 0 X

Laserprinted paperback coordinated in UK by Laserbacks, 11 Rosemont Road, London NW3 6NG

# INTRODUCTION

For almost two thousand years most of Jesus' Life has been shrouded in complete mystery, little or nothing being known about his childhood or youth. A fact which must have intrigued millions of Christians the world over for centuries past.

How was it possible that so little information concerning his early life had been handed down to us, when his birth and the last few years of his earthly life were so well documented? The truth is that men have ever been nationalistic and arrogant and when the early stories of Christ were passed on, much was deliberately omitted. Even Jesus himself, knowing well the natures and minds of men, knew better than to antagonise his fellow countrymen with references to earlier years spend in Egypt and Persia.

The story of Jesus as told in this book blends information taken from the four Gospels, with revelations made by Hafed, Arch Magi of Persia, who is better known to Christians as one of the three Magi of biblical fame.

It was in November, 1869 that the spirit of Hafed first communicated with a small group of men investigating psychic phenomena who were conducting a seance in Glasgow with a local medium named David Duguid, and although Hafed's importance was not immediately perceived, once established that he was none other than leader of the three famous Magi who had paid homage to the infant Jesus in Bethlehem, then everything he uttered was carefully recorded.

Hafed was to speak to the group no less than one hundred times during the next four years, and in 1875 the written notes were published in the form of a book entitled *Hafed, a Prince of Persia* which was to become a best-seller.

*The Glasgow Christian News* dated February 19th, 1876, was to declare 'Remarkable...a phenomenon to be accounted for...All Christian ministers should make themselves fully acquainted with Hafed that they might be able to deal suitably with it as occasion may arise. Multitudes of the young and not a few of the old, in Christian congregations will, as time rolls on, come to hear of Hafed and to read it, and its influence on their minds will not be slight.'

In London the *Spiritual Magazine* for February 1876 was to state 'The communications are of the most marvellous character, and if accepted as genuine throw a flood of light upon a period of history of which we know little, and to which more interest attaches than to any other. The medium through whom these communications have been made is well known, at least by name, wherever spiritualism has gained a footing, mainly for the extraordinary pictures which he has painted while in a state of trance. He is an ordinary, uneducated, simple-minded, plain working man, with not the slightest pretension to any knowledge of ancient history, or of the subjects generally treated of in this volume, and we know personally David Duguid; and of this fact we are certain that unaided by any power outside of his own mind, he could no more have answered the questions put to him in the form in which they are answered in this volume than he could have written Bacon's Organon, Newton's Principles or Shakespeare's plays'...'What Hafed has to say, therefore, must be looked upon as of the greatest possible importance. If this be true, it has an interest for us greater than the contents of any other book outside the holy Scriptures'.

In the United States the *Religion Philosophical Journal* of Chicago on the 4th of March, 1876 was to declare 'Literature has nothing equal to this marvellous narrative'.

Regardless of the praise heaped upon this astonishing book and its disclosures however, Victorian and Edwardian Britain was too strongly in the grip of religious orthodoxy for the book to achieve any lasting impact, and in the years that were to follow virtually all copies were to disappear. One man has recently testified that he had spent FORTY YEARS trying to locate a copy, even enlisting the services of a 'book world search' organisation without success. Just how the book was to emerge again in the 1980s is a story that is as astonishing as the original revelations, and this time I myself was to be the instrument for their revival.

Completely unaware that the 'Hafed' book had ever existed, I was one day told by a spirit voice that I was to 'Help in the writing of a most important book' At the time I wondered what precisely was meant by 'help', but was too awe-struck to enquire. I was also informed that I would meet 'Three men dressed in black who will lead you to the next stage of your spiritual adventure'.

Many months later I DID meet these men in the church of St. Bartholomew the Great at Smithfield, London, and during a conversation with one of them was told about the book of Hafed, and it was suggested that I should try to obtain a copy, although I was warned that it could take many months or even years before I was able to locate a copy.

The following day I commenced to search amongst the many bookshops that lined London's Charing Cross Road, however no one had ever heard of the book I wanted. After visiting some fifteen or sixteen shops without success, I was about to give up the search for that particular day, when to my astonishment I heard my own voice declaring to one shopkeeper 'The book concerns the missing years in the life of Christ'—the shopkeeper had just stated that he really had no idea of what I was looking for—I had forgotten the title. Now, suddenly, he declared 'Ah, then I DO have the book you want. Someone sold it to me only a FEW MINUTES AGO,' and as they handed it to me remarked 'It is about the missing years in the life of Christ'.

Having bought and read the book, I knew instinctively the part I had to play. I must revise and edit the contents so as to make the book more readable for a modern public. This I did in the months that followed, and it was published under its original title in December, 1987 by Regency Press (London & New York) Ltd.

Later it occurred to me that I should produce another book blending Hafed's information with a single narration of the four Gospels, together with explanations for many of the psychic events which occurred during our Lord's life on earth—something I venture to say can only be done by someone who possesses true spiritual awareness. Most churchmen may well have abundant religious knowledge, but sadly they all too often reveal a dismal lack of spiritual understanding or awareness.

I therefore hope that this little book will not only give all true followers of Jesus a new insight into his earthly life, but a greater understanding of all things spiritual. It should be clearly understood that the spiritual world is not simply something that affects us when we 'pass on'—the world of spirit surrounds us HERE AND NOW. It should also be understood that the world of spirit is no wispy, transparent illusion as so many would like to believe, everything in its own dimension being as 'solid' as objects would appear to be to us in this, our material world.

For all their technical skills and advances in the 20th century, our men of science have barely scratched the surface of true knowledge.

Ronald Wright

CONTENTS

# 1

## *The angel speaks to Mary*

In the days of Herod, king of Judaea, there was a certain priest named Zacharias. He and his wife Elizabeth were a very pious and kindly couple, the one great disappointment of their life being that they were childless and, at the time of which I speak, Elizabeth had grown much too old to bear a child.

But it came to pass that one day when Zacharias was doing his duties in the synagogue, an angel suddenly appeared before him. Filled with wonder and fear, Zacharias stood trembling as he gazed upon the bright being. 'Fear not,' said the angel, 'for thy prayers have been heard, and thy wife Elizabeth shall bear thee a son, and thou shalt call him John. Many shall rejoice in his birth, for he shall become great in the sight of the Lord. He shall drink neither wine nor strong drink, and shall be filled with the Holy Spirit, causing many in Israel to mend their ways and return to the Lord their God.'

Having recovered from his initial shock at seeing the angel, Zacharias said, 'How can this be?...both my wife and I are far too old to have children now!' But the angel replied, 'I am Gabriel, that stands in the presence of God, and have been sent to inform you of these glad tidings, and I assure you that it shall be as I have said. However since you have seen fit to doubt my words, you shall be struck dumb until the day when this thing shall come to pass.' So saying, the angel disappeared and Zacharias found that he had indeed lost his power to speak.

Time passed, and Elizabeth discovered to her great joy that she *was* with child...'How good the Lord has been to me,' said Elizabeth, adding 'now I need no longer be ashamed that I am barren among women.'

Six months later the angel Gabriel visited the town of Nazareth, going to the home of Mary a young virgin who had recently become engaged to a local carpenter named Joseph, a direct descendant of the House of David. At the sight of the dazzling being, Mary was filled with wonder and astonishment. Then said the angel to her, 'Hail, thou that art highly favoured. The Lord is with thee. Blessed art thou among women.' Then seeing how the young maid trembled with fear the angel said, 'Fear not Mary, for thou hast found favour with God, and behold, thou shalt conceive in thy womb and bring forth a son, and thou shalt call his name Jesus. He shall become great and shall be called the son of the highest, and the Lord God shall give unto him the throne of his father David, and he shall reign over the House of Jacob for ever, and of his kingdom there shall be no end.'

Then said Mary to the angel, 'How can this be when I am unmarried and have never known (sexually) a man?' But the angel replied, 'The Holy Spirit shall come upon thee, and the power of Almighty God shall enter thee, so that the child you shall bring forth shall be the son of God. Know also that thy cousin Elizabeth who was so old and barren, has conceived a son, and is in the sixth month with the child. Nothing is impossible for God.'

Then said Mary to the angel, 'Behold the handmaid of the Lord...His will be done,' and the angel departed from her.

A few days later Mary decided to pay a visit to her elderly cousin Elizabeth, who lived in Judaea. Having entered the house, she greeted her cousin, who immediately felt her baby leap within her, and remarked, 'Oh Mary, how marvellous it is that God has blessed us both in this way, and how great an honour God has bestowed upon you, to single you out from all other women of the world to bear His earthly son.'

Mary stayed with Elizabeth for three months before returning home to Nazareth.

Great was the rejoicing when Elizabeth eventually gave birth to her son, and all her relations and friends gathered at the house to celebrate the blessed event.

When the baby was eight days old, he was taken to the synagogue to be circumcised. All the relatives assumed that the child would be named Zacharias after his father, and were surprised when Elizabeth said, 'He is to be called John.' Turning to Zacharias, they made signs asking what name he wished the child to have (you will recall the angel Gabriel had struck him dumb). Zacharias indicated he wanted something to write on, and having been handed a tablet wrote, 'His name is to be John.' Almost immediately his speech was restored, and filled with the Holy Spirit Zacharias began to prophecy in a loud voice saying, 'Blessed be the Lord God of Israel. Praised be the Lord for sending to us one who is to save and redeem his people, one who like the great prophets of the past shall save us from our enemies and all those who hate us. One who shall give the great mercies promised to our fathers, and shall remember God's holy Covenant, sworn to our ancestor Abraham, that we should be delivered out of the hands of our enemies, and serve God without fear in holiness and righteousness all the days of our lives.'

Then addressing the child Zacharias said, 'And thou, child, shall be called the prophet of the highest, for it shall be thy task to prepare a pathway for him who God shall send. Thou shalt preach to the people that salvation shall come to them through the remission of their sins. Thou shalt give them light in their darkness, and guide their feet along the pathway of peace.'

And when the people had listened to Zacharias' prophecy, they wondered what kind of man this tiny babe would grow into. As the child grew older it was seen that he was indeed filled with the Holy Spirit, and by the time he was a young man, his fame as a fiery evangelist preacher became known both near and far. Choosing a life as near to nature as possible, he made his home in the desert wilderness, and lived on locusts and honey.

# 2

## *Birth of Jesus: Visit of the Magi*

In the meantime young Mary had married Joseph the carpenter, knowing that the child she carried within her had been created by the Holy Spirit, and as the time for the birth drew near, a decree from the Emperor Caesar Augustus went out that a census of all the Roman world should take place. Since this required that all men should register in their place of origin, Joseph in company with his wife set out for Bethlehem, in Judaea.

On arrival, the first thing Joseph did was try to find suitable accommodation for his young wife, who was now so heavy with child. Wearily they went to all the inns and lodging houses in the town, only to be told at each place...'Sorry, we have no room.' Eventually however, one inn-keeper suggested they seek shelter in a cattle shed at the rear of his inn...here at least they would have a roof over their heads.

The following night, some shepherds were attending to their flocks on the hills just outside Bethlehem, when suddenly a dazzling angel appeared to them. At first the shepherds were terror-stricken, but the angel said, 'Fear not, for unto you this night I bring the most wonderful news, news that in time shall benefit all mankind. For unto you this day has been born in the city of David, a Saviour which is Christ the Lord. Seek, and you shall find the babe wrapped in swaddling clothes, lying in a manger.'

The next moment the whole sky above the shepherds appeared to be filled with bright angels, all praising God and saying, 'Glory to God in the highest, and on earth peace and good-will towards all men.' Then, just as suddenly as the angels had appeared, so they vanished, leaving the bewildered shepherds to stare at each other in utter amazement. When they had sufficiently recovered their senses, they said to each other, 'Let us go into the town, find this child the angel spoke of, and worship him.'

At the same time the shepherds were heading for the town to seek Jesus, so also were three wise men (Magi) from the land of Persia; they were Hafed, Arch-Magus of Persia, and two of his Brethren, Pacorus and Cofdraes. They too had been instructed by a bright spirit (the Spirit of Light) that they must seek Jesus and pay homage to him. The bright spirit had told them that he himself would guide them to the spot where they should find this King of Kings and Lord of Lords, saying that he would guide them as a star by night, and a strongly-felt presence by day. Before commencing their journey, the Spirit of Light gave them a casket of jewels (specially materialised before them) which they were to give to Mary and Joseph to sell as and when the need should arise.

As the three Magi neared the great and magnificent city of Jerusalem, they felt that surely this was an appropriate birth-place for such a personage as they sought. So ignoring the guiding spirit which had brought them this far, on entering the city they went straight to King Herod's palace and asked where the Messiah might be found, that they might pay homage to him. When Herod heard this he was greatly troubled, fearing his throne to be in danger. Calling all his chief priests and scribes together, he demanded they tell him where Christ was to be born. They told him that it was written in the ancient records of many countries that, 'thou O Bethlehem, in the land of Judaea shall not be least among the Princes (cities) of that country, for out of thee shall come one who will rule thy people, Israel.'

Hearing this, the king immediately summoned the three Magi into his presence and told them to seek for the young child in Bethlehem, requesting that when they had in fact located him, they should return to Jerusalem and report his whereabouts so that he, Herod, might himself pay respects to the young Prince. Having promised to do so, the Magi departed, but they had not gone far before the bright spirit appeared before them once more. After rebuking them for following the dictates of their own minds and entering Jerusalem, instead of following his guidance, the Spirit said that the child they sought would not be found in splendid palaces such as they had visited in the city. The Spirit added that he was aware that Herod had made them promise to return to him as soon as they had seen the child, but on no account were they to do so, for Herod's only interest was to destroy the babe, not worship him. Then in a vision the heavenly messenger showed them the terrible slaughter of innocent children which would follow their visit to Bethlehem, and they knew their promise to Herod was not binding in heaven.

Eventually the Magi reached Bethlehem, and found the child they sought, not in a marble palace, but in a lowly cattle shed, smiling in the lap of his young mother. Having paid homage to the child, Hafed, the Arch-Magus warned Joseph that Herod was seeking to destroy the child, and for their safety said they should flee to Egypt with all possible haste. Handing Joseph the casket of jewels given to him by the Spirit of Light, Hafed said the jewels could be bartered for safe conduct to Egypt and to relieve their poverty. Hafed then explained that Joseph should take his little family to the ancient city of Thebes, wherein one of the temples there he would find an old priest named Issha, who would not only help them to find a home in the city, but would undertake the education of the young child as soon as he was old enough.

Their task completed, the three Magi returned once more to Persia, being careful to avoid Jerusalem and heading for the Red Sea where they intended to board a ship for their homeland.

Having been alerted to the dangers facing them, Joseph made preparations to leave as soon as his wife had sufficiently recovered, but before commencing the long journey to Egypt, he and Mary took the child to a synagogue, so that it might be circumcised according to custom. As they entered the synagogue, a certain devout and spiritually developed old man named Simeon came forward and begged that he might be allowed to hold the baby for a moment. The parents gave their permission, and taking the young child in his old arms he then said loudly, 'Lord, now may I die in peace, for thou hast kept the promise made to me that mine eyes should be allowed to see the salvation thou had prepared for all the peoples of the earth.'

Mary and Joseph were quite astounded that the old man should be aware of the Baby's origin and future, and realised at once that the old man must be a spirit medium. Bestowing his blessings on the couple, the old man said to Mary, ' This child is destined for greatness...many shall rise and fall on his account and you, Mary, shall pay the price of bitter pain and sadness, that the will of God may be accomplished through this little one.'

There was also present in the synagogue that day, another aged medium, a woman known as Anna, who spent much of her time in deep prayer and spiritual trance. She too was aware of the child's destiny, likewise she also blessed Jesus and told others present that here was the future Saviour of Israel. When the service of circumcision had been completed, the holy family immediately left for Egypt.

# 3

## *The child grows up in Egypt*

As planned, the Magi reached the Red Sea and took ship for Persia, but as they neared Aden they were chased by pirates and had to seek refuge on the western shore of the sea. Having landed, Hafed the Arch-Magus and his Brethren decided to journey to Thebes in order that they might fore-warn the old Egyptian priest Issha, that the holy family would shortly be arriving.

Incidentally, one should not imagine that because most Egyptian priests and the mass of the Egyptian people bent the knee to the figures and images within their temples, that there were not those who worshipped the One God, the Creator and Sustainer of all things. Indeed there were many among the learned, and old Issha was perhaps the most devout.

Having arrived in Thebes, the Magi were given a great welcome by the old Egyptian priest who, on learning of the reason for their mission, raised his aged eyes to heaven and thanked the great and Holy Spirit that he had been spared to hail the advent of the long-promised Deliverer. While giving eloquent expression to the feelings of his gratified soul, the temple trembled as if shaken by an earthquake, and a voice was heard to say...'Issha, thou hast been kept alive for heaven's purpose. The child will be brought hither, and he shall be guarded by thee. Thou shalt show him all the sacred symbols, so that he may be instructed in these, till the time comes when the spirit shall guide him.' The ancient priest stood as erect as a youth, so gladdened was he by the tidings the Magi had brought, and their wonderful confirmation from the unseen.

The temple, to which the holy family were now progressing, was known as the sacred temple, and was hewn out of solid rock, the roof supported by most gorgeously wrought columns cut from the same rock. Having no windows, the temple was lighted by many lamps which hung from the roof, and the whole interior was beautifully adorned with ornaments of gold and silver. All who entered the temple immediately sensed the holiness of the place, and so magnetised was the atmosphere therein, that a thrill shot over the whole body of all who entered. And well it might be so, for here it was that the priests received the Oracles (spirit messages) from the unseen world, and here it was that God had chosen Jesus should receive the first phase of his education.

By the time the holy family had actually arrived in Thebes, the Magi had left, and were well on their way home to Persia once more. Jesus was accepted into the temple as soon as he was able to walk and talk, and his parents having taken a house nearby, were able to visit him whenever they wished. Joseph resuming his craft as a carpenter in the city.

Writing to Hafed in Persia some time later, old Issha had this to say of his young charge: 'The child, though but three years old, shows in his ways so much that is God-like that I could almost fall down and worship him. Those who attend on him say that never was such a child as this little one committed to my care. To think that one so young in years, should come to hoary age (Issha was nearly a hundred years old) and put questions so deep that to answer them would puzzle a Socrates or a Plato, is indeed very wonderful to me. And often times I am astonished when he asks me the meaning of some of our sacred symbols, and about other things far above a child's capacity'.

A year later when Jesus was then four years old, Issha sent another letter to Hafed via one of the many caravans of merchants that regularly traded between their countries, and in this he said: 'Most noble Hafed, servant of the Living God and Prince of Persia. In this, my second epistle, I have unspeakable pleasure in giving thee some fuller account of my young charge. O that dear one, how I reverence him. I cannot help it. Old as I am, as I said before, I could almost fall down at the feet of the beloved child and worship him. It is something very wonderful to see, this little one pacing along the dark and solemn recesses of our inner temple—those silent floors, where even the oldest priest dare not venture alone. Yet he, the wondrous child, dares to look into the holy place. holy indeed it is when he is there. He is clever beyond all other children; for he hath gained already some knowledge of ancient languages, and listens with deep attention while I am instructing him on the history of this country—of its great fame in years gone by for wisdom and power, and how the race from which he sprang had been fed and benefited, and afterwards enslaved by the rulers of Egypt. But much of that history is now lost...thanks to Persia for that, for it was a Persian king that destroyed our ancient records.

'I have heard thee speak of spirit communicating in thought with men, and truly it must be so with this little one, for the most intricate passages in our hieroglyphs, if once he gets the key, he deciphers with ease. That certain passage, the meaning of which has been to thee and to me a source of much dispute and trouble, has been clearly revealed by him. I believe him to be indeed the son of God, having in him the Spirit of the Father'.

Issha's letter continued with some personal news relating to his own life, then returned once more to the subject of Jesus, relating how at the age of four he had performed his first miracle: 'A poor man, who had once been rich and paid largely to the temple service, having lost all and become maimed by an encounter with pirates on the Red Sea, was carried one day in his helpless state into the temple about the time for evening worship. The young child stood by his side, and seeing this maimed old man in his pitiable condition, he looked up to me and said, 'Father,' (he always calleth me Father) 'this poor old man must have a history.' and then, wonderful to tell, he narrated the chief points in the old man's life. Then going up to where he crouched, Jesus said, 'Rise!'

'But how can I rise...I have no power,' said the poor man.

Stretching out his tiny hand towards him, the child uttered the word 'Rise!' And up started the old man, standing on his feet with all his wonted vigour. Here was power displayed of a truly wonderful kind. But there are many other things done by him which show him to be so full of love. Even the other little ones, the children of the priests, never have cause in their play to chide him. Wherever he is there is happiness and peace, and all goes well'.

Yet another letter sent from Issha to Hafed two years later when Jesus was then six years old, contains the following passages:

'Most noble Hafed, servant of the Living God, ambassador of heaven, chosen to proclaim the birth and do homage to him who is the son of God-Honoured wert thou, my noble brother, to bend the knee and present rich gifts to the holy child; who, though born in a lowly place, was mightier far than any of the princes of the world. The Hebrews boast of their great and wise kings; but what is their wisest compared with Jesus, my prince? Nothing. I take delight once more in writing to you concerning him. He is growing in stature, and daily he shows an increase in wisdom; indeed, he puts us all to shame by the depth of his remarks on subjects beyond our reach. When asked to give a decision, he is always ready, and wonderful are his judgments.

'This young and growing Light is beginning to dispel the darkness that hovers around our sacred buildings. Strange to say, in many cases he is the teacher and I am the taught, and I am not ashamed to own this to thee, my friend. When sitting with me in my lonely cell at night, he will make the strangest revelations of the unseen world. We, as priests, have learned and heard much about such things. But this little one talks of heaven, and opens up paradise in all its glory and beauty...telling me of things not spoken of on earth. He told me also of enemies who were seeking to destroy my influence as a priest; 'but be not afraid,' he said, 'for there are many around to bear thee up.' When I contrast the wisdom of Egypt with the sayings of this child, the one is far surpassed by the other. We have travelled in Egypt, and visited other temples and witnessed the religious services engaged therein. Such mummeries, however, are no longer practised here; for how shall man with the light of truth around him, bend the knee to a reptile! Oh, how often have I in my darkness bowed low before a dumb fowl. I abhor myself now. And yet, when we reflect, must not man, even in his gross darkness, worship that which he considers likest to God? In the case of the Greeks, they make their Gods in the likeness of man. This seems in advance of other nations. But as I look on this boy, I see the Divine spirit flashing from his eyes, giving light to my dim orbs.

'I must tell you, we were engaged one day in speaking of the Great and Mighty Spirit, when overhearing the question of a bystander...'Which was true God?'...he said it was time we gave up bending before these idols. But I told him they were looked upon by us merely as symbols, to which he replied that God was to be worshipped according to the way laid down in the Jewish books. I said, how do you know that? He said that his mother told him. He pointed his finger to passages, penned hundreds of years before concerning his birth, Herod's cruel edict and the flight into Egypt. This was all (said the child) foreseen by God; and by the prophets who declared it, he thus forewarned the people; but man rejected the warning. 'I come not,' said this little one, 'to overthrow thrones and kingdoms...I come to overthrow the evil in the hearts of men...to point them to heaven and lead them in the right way.' Then we talked of the dealings of God with the ancestors of the Hebrew nation and their escape from Egyptian bondage...of the deliverance of the Hebrews and the engulfing of Pharaoh and his host in the Red Sea. Was God an angry God...revenging himself on his adversaries? 'No,' he said, 'it was the simple result of Pharaoh's foolhardiness. Put thy finger on the flame and thou wilt be burned. So with the Egyptian host. And yet for all this, Egypt is not wholly forgotten. That same land which became a nursing mother to the famishing Israelites, my Father sends me to, that I may also be nursed by her.'

Concluding his letter to Hafed, Issha has this to say: 'I must tell thee that there has come to us three priests from lesser Egypt to confer with me in regard to religion. They had heard from others of my change of mind in regard to the prevailing opinions; and they want to sit in council on the matter. Thou wilt know the result when we meet. But we are all at one here in our religious ideas...even the strong-headed priests are imbibing the truth. Great is the change, which thou wilt be informed of ere long. I leave thee now for a while. May the Great the Mighty Spirit ever abide with thee, and may His presence be ever felt in all our ways'.

# 4

## *Jesus is taken to Persia*

Two years later, when Jesus was eight years old, Issha decided to take him on a visit to Hafed in Persia, and so it was that after the rainy season, and before the hot season began, they departed from Egypt in company with a band of Persian merchants about to leave for their homeland.

It was during this journey, that Issha was once more to have evidence that the young boy in his charge was truly the son of Almighty God, for only a short time after the caravan of merchants had set out, they were attacked by a horde of robbers. In the disorder that ensued, Issha and the young Jesus were suddenly lifted up from the earth, and conveyed along by some unseen power. On and on they were carried, out of danger, and out of Egypt, across deserts and mountains, eventually to be set down in Persia but a short distance from their destination. Their extraordinary transportation had quite astounded Issha, the young Jesus however seemed to take the whole thing quite calmly, knowing in fact exactly who the powers were that conveyed them, since he spoke with them several times during the amazing journey.

In the meantime Hafed and other members of the Magi were at prayer in the sacred grove...the Magi worshipped not in buildings of stone created by men, but in leafy groves surrounded by nature and the works of God. As they prayed silently around the altar which stood in the centre of the grove, the Messenger of God called the Spirit of Light suddenly appeared before them and said, 'Why tarry ye here? One more worthy of your homage awaits you outside the grove. Go forth and welcome the Prince of heaven and earth.'

The Magi were greatly surprised by this announcement, for although the visit of Jesus and Issha was expected, they knew that the caravan of merchants with whom they were travelling was not due for some considerable time yet. Nevertheless, at the bidding of the spirit they went forth, and once outside the grove they saw some distance away the venerable old priest approaching, with the little boy running along at his side.

The Magi went forward to meet them and on drawing near, Hafed fell on his knees before Issha. 'Nay, my son, rise to thy feet,' said the old priest, 'it becomes me rather to do homage to thee, for have I not received treasures of truth and light, and above all, been honoured in having had so long a time the care of this child...it is HE who is worthy of thy homage.'

Their greetings exchanged, Hafed enquired how came they so quickly to complete their journey, and Issha related the amazing story of their transportation by unseen spirits, Issha remarking that young Jesus seemed not only to enjoy the experience, but to know the identity of those spirits who carried them, for the child had spoken names he had often referred to in the temple.

Since the little boy seemed instantly to recognize Hafed, the Arch Magus asked the child if he had seen him before, to which Jesus replied, 'Yes. When my aged father sent letters to thee, I saw thee reading them.' Another proof that the child was indeed the Great One, long promised in the ancient records of Egypt, Persia, Israel, and indeed over all the East.

Then Hafed spoke to Jesus saying, 'It shall be my duty to give thee all the knowledge that I am able to impart; but thou, beloved, hast that within thee that to which I or my brethren cannot attain. Nevertheless, I shall endeavour to teach thee.' But then, feeling his own weakness Hafed prayed, 'O, Almighty Father of spirits, source of all truth, enable me, by the help of thy ministering angels, to become the teacher and guide of thy son, the long-promised Deliverer.'

It being the custom of the Magi to hold a festival whenever visited by any distinguished strangers, such was immediately called for, the feast consisting not of meats and wines, but herbs, fruit and pure spring-water. Sitting in the open air, Issha and the young Jesus were placed in a circle formed by the principal Magi, outside of which were other circles, composed of the brethren according to their station in the order, while outside these circles were first the holy women and wives of the Magi, and then the children. A lamb, decorated with fresh flowers, emblem of innocence and purity, was then placed in the space between the various circles, and each one who had children, in turn, laid their hands on the lamb, vowing to bring up their offspring in a knowledge of the true God. After partaking of the fruits, both fresh and preserved, and drinking of pure water, the elder Magi welcomes Jesus and Issha to the holy circle, after which the official address was given.

The Persian Religion at that time believed in a three-fold manifestation of the Godhead, and this formed at all times a subject for their deepest meditation. But now, here stood one in their midst whom they looked upon as the son of God, the Prince, the Leader so long promised to man for every epistle sent from the venerable old Egyptian priest, Issha, had been read to the assembled Magi, who were accordingly prepared to receive this visit, and very much did they venerate the holy man for his work and his labour of love.

# 5

## *Jesus in care of the Magi*

The Festival now at an end, the young Jesus was committed to the care of Hafed the Arch Magus, who proceeded to instruct his young pupil in Persian literature and theology, as well as the manners and customs of the country his future public ministry, and it was in accordance with the mind of the Great Spirit that, as a preparation for the work, he should know the trials that mankind were subjected to, not merely the trials of the physical life, but those which affect men spiritually also.

Hafed quickly discovered that his young charge had been well taught by old Issha, not only in the theology of Egypt, but that of the Hebrews also, for Egypt was at that time in the possession of one of the best translations of the Hebrew records—the work of Jewish scribes, who became dwellers in Egypt after the death of Alexander the Great, when his kingdom was divided. Issha had instructed Jesus in the prophecies concerning himself, as these were found in the Hebrew books, and day after day he was to receive confirmation of these from the Spirit in the sacred grove of the Magi.

At last the time came when Issha should return to his native land, leaving the young Jesus in the tender care of Hafed. The Magi having assembled to bid Issha farewell, the old man thanked them for their hospitality, then embracing first Hafed, and then Jesus, he spoke to the child saying, 'Farewell, my beautiful, my darling son—thou who instructed me! The time cometh when thou shalt tread that land which hath cast thee out, and there shalt thou kindle a flame which will lighten the world. Though I go now to Egypt and there die, I will in spirit aid thee in the trials and troubles that will assuredly come upon thee. I am not afraid to leave thee with my friend Hafed. He will instruct thee in the knowledge of many things that will be good for thee, my son, to learn. So, farewell! When I leave this frail body thou wilt know it. We shall meet again.'

With those words he fell on the neck of Hafed and wept. Then as Issha parted from his old friend, he grasped young Jesus, and holding him aloft to God, he cried out, 'The charge committed to me I now deliver up. Behold, with Thy help I have done my duty. For I know thou art ever near me. I thank and adore Thee, O Great and good. Bless all around me, as Thou seest they need. God of love and peace, but not war, Thou who hast done so much for me, carry me back in peace to my own land, that there I may take my leave of my friends and brethren before I cast off this frail body. And when free, O Great Father, enable me to come back in spirit.'

The farewells concluded, Issha joined a caravan of merchants and departed. For the rest of that day Jesus was somewhat downcast, but by the next day he was diligently applying himself to the studies that Hafed had set before him. Under the instruction of the Arch Magus, he soon acquired a knowledge of the Persian language, religion, and law, to such an extent and in so short a time, that all the brethren were astounded. Hafed also opened up the doctrines of Zoroaster to Jesus, revealed the mysteries of the Magi, and taught him all he knew about natural laws. A study was also made of the supernatural, with which all the Magi were acquainted, though not all were as advanced in spirit communion (mediumship) as others.

The tireless way in which the young Jesus applied himself to all his studies, and the profound wisdom which the child displayed soon astonished the Magi, and in fact so great an impression did he make on them that he was even admitted to the centre altar in the sacred grove...the first child ever to look upon that holy place. But the heavenly spirit who came frequently to the sacred grove knew Jesus, and many were the things of the spirit world which they discussed.

One morning—glorious summer morning—while the sun was gliding the plains with golden hues and the Magi were all engaged in their usual morning worship, Jesus strayed from the grove and wandered into the fields beyond. Here he met with an old shepherd in a great state of anxiety, and seeing the evident distress on the old man's face, the child asked what was the matter. The shepherd replied that some of his lambs were missing and he feared that they must have been carried off by wild animals. To the astonishment of the old man, the child said, 'Why did you neglect your flock, and allow your lambs to stray? But, know that they are safe. There is one above who careth for your lambs. Go forward to yonder hill and there you shall find them.' Going as the child had directed, the shepherd did indeed find his lost lambs, and great was his rejoicing. When he returned home, the shepherd related to his neighbours the story of the remarkable child he had encountered. The subject excited a great deal of general interest so that eventually even the king came to hear of it and requested that Jesus be sent to him.

Not long after this, Hafed and a group of the Magi were out walking in the countryside one evening, when they came across a large assembly of people. As they drew nearer, they were amazed to see the young Jesus, perched upon the stones of an old altar, addressing the people. He spoke of the worlds above, and the bright mansions prepared for the spirits of the good, and of his Father's love for all.

He called on the people to bring forth their sick that they might be healed. As the Magi drew nearer still, a sight met Hafed's gaze that he was never to forget. Blinking his eyes in disbelief, he thought at first his eyes must be deceiving him, for there, standing beside the young Jesus was the familiar figure of his friend Issha, the old Egyptian priest, habited in white, and appearing to dictate every word which the child was uttering. Overjoyed, Hafed ran forward to embrace his old friend, but as he did so, Issha seemed to simply melt away. Amazed, Hafed enquired of Jesus if his old friend really had been present. 'Yes,' answered Jesus, 'but he is in the spirit. He will meet you again at midnight in the sacred grove.' Explaining that Issha had died immediately after returning to Egypt, Jesus then stepped down from the altar. Had any one but those belonging to the sacred order of the Magi dared to have occupied the same position, it would have meant death; such was the veneration shown by the people for the sacredness of the altar, but they had been wonder-struck and no one had dared to touch the boy.

Now Hafed mounted the steps of the altar and spoke to the assembled people 'People of Persia, you have been highly blessed this day. The son of God has appeared before you. Be not afraid, I am not turning away from my old faith.' And then he told them how he and two brethren had been commissioned from the highest to welcome the birth of the Prince of Peace, and spoke of the great mission and work he was destined to accomplish in the world. While he thus spoke, the people cried and said, 'It is true! it is true!' and declared the extraordinary cures he had been making, and many of his wonderful sayings and doings.

# 6

## *Jesus shows Hafed the glory of his kingdom*

Having received a letter from Jesus' parents in Egypt requesting that he be sent back to them, Hafed resolved to return with the child himself, and to go by way of Greece since his young charge earnestly desired some insight into the manners and customs of those people whose history and literature Hafed had opened up to him. Joseph the carpenter having heard that King Herod was now dead, (the Magi had also received news through the spirit in the grove) had decided it was right that Jesus should now return to Judaea. Certainly that country was sorely in need of a deliverer—murder, rapine and every kind of evil being rampant everywhere.

The fame of the youth had by this time spread all over Persia. From the king downwards all loved him, for he always had a kind word and a helping hand for all whom he met, and when it became known that he was about to depart from Persia for his own land, presents from people of all walks of life poured in to him. Poor he may have been on arrival in Persia a few years earlier, but now he was to leave it greatly enriched. Rich indeed, in mental gifts had he already been when he came from Egypt, now he left Persia endowed with all the additional learning which the Magi could instil.

At length the day arrived when Jesus, accompanied by Hafed should leave. Early in the morning the Magi Brethren held a service in the sacred grove, offering up prayers to the Great and good Creator, the Father of all, and Father of the young boy bending the knee with them before the sacred altar. The service over, Jesus and Hafed together with several attendants set off on camels for the start of their journey. As evening drew near, they came to a grove of trees with a small stream gushing through it, and having refreshed themselves at the stream, they decided to make camp for the night in the shelter of the trees.

As Jesus and Hafed lay beneath the great canopy of the star-bespangled sky, they talked about the spirit world, and wonderfully did Jesus describe his previous existence there. He also spoke concerning many of the stars which sparkled so brightly over their heads, and Hafed who had previously considered he himself to have been very knowledgeable on the subject, realised that the child knew much more. Then, as they lay quietly communing, the very heavens themselves seemed to open up before them. At first Hafed had thought he must be dreaming, but then he realised that this was not the case—he was wide awake and fully conscious. It was as though they had been transferred (teleported) to another world, and there before them stood a city of such dazzling beauty and brightness that nothing on earth could possibly be compared with it. As they drew near, Hafed saw that the streets of the city were thronged with hosts of glorified spirits, all clothed in flowing robes of white, and all emitting a dazzling brightness which eclipsed even the glory of the spirit in the sacred grove with which he was familiar.

Ahead, and towering above them, there came into view a might temple, with walls of crystal and precious stones of such dazzling beauty and strength as no earthly hand was capable of constructing. Entering the magnificent building, Hafed saw a splendid throne, and around the interior as far as the eyes could see stood thousands upon thousands of holy spirits, whose countenances reflected the light shining forth from the throne. Seeing all this, he was awe-struck, and when Jesus turned to him and said, 'Father, yonder is my throne,' Hafed could not help expressing his belief that Jesus was more than mortal, to which the youth replied, 'Nay my father, I am just such as you are, but I was before you. I will return to this bright abode before you are taken away, but in due time you shall meet me here. Now you have beheld my throne, and you will yet see me seated thereon to give judgment to the kings of the earth.'

As they turned to leave the temple, Hafed to his great joy saw once again the bright spirit-form of his old friend Issha, standing on the steps of the entrance. Moments later, his astral projection at an end, Hafed's spiritual self had returned once more to inhabit its earthly shell, and he found himself once again gazing up at the starry sky above, lying with Jesus at his side.

# 7

## *Jesus at the temple in Jerusalem*

After an uneventful journey to Greece, Hafed and his young charge went on to visit Rome before finally setting sail for Egypt. Arriving at the sacred temple in Thebes, Hafed and Jesus went first to the grave of their old friend, Issha (he had left instructions that his body was to be buried, not embalmed) so that they might pay homage to his memory. Then finding that Jesus' parents had already departed for Judaea some time before, Hafed and Jesus spent a few days visiting and speaking with old friends in Thebes. Then they set off on their travels once more, this time to Nazareth.

Wonderful was the welcome they received when finally they arrived, and after so long a separation it was only natural that the parents of Jesus, and his brothers and sisters, should all have a great many questions they wished to put to him relating to his journeys.

It had been about the time of the Passover when they had arrived, and as was the custom, great numbers of people from Judaea were going up to Jerusalem to observe it. Jesus and his parents went too, and Hafed accompanied them since he was desirous of coming into contact with the learned people he hoped to find there. Having arrived in the city, Hafed and Jesus (now 12 years old) sought the place where the learned teachers of the people gathered to discuss various questions of a religious character. Though taking no part themselves, Hafed and Jesus listened with great interest, and Hafed was glad of the opportunity afforded his young companion of coming into contact with men who, in Hebrew literature and religion, were capable of adding to the instruction which he had endeavoured to instil into his pupil, regarding the history and faith of his own countrymen. Attending each day with increasing interest, they listened to many topics upon which Hafed could not be expected to be so well informed as the Jewish doctors.

Towards the end of the Passover, the parents of Jesus expressed their intention of leaving the city and returning home, whereupon before parting from them, Hafed said he would like to pay a visit to the place where Jesus had first seen the light of the earthly sphere, and there pray and meditate on the many wonderful things that had transpired since then. Having visited Bethlehem, Hafed returned once more to Jerusalem, arriving one day before Passover ended. Going to the temple as was his custom, Hafed was surprised to find young Jesus still there (Hafed had left him in the care of his parents), standing in the midst of a group of learned disputants, putting such questions and giving such answers as to fairly silence these venerable Fathers of the Hebrew nation. Hafed smiled as he gazed on their dumfounded faces, for where had this boy learned such a knowledge of things? His teaching must have come from the spirit world...they were not of earth. Only the Great and Holy Spirit could have been the source of what flowed forth from the child. Hafed took no part in the discussion; he was so entranced he could say nothing and was amused as he watched these grey-haired venerable men sitting powerless before this mere child.

When the discussion was ended, Hafed went up to Jesus to enquire about his parents and discovered that they had already left the city...unaware that Jesus was not with them. Hafed therefore proposed that they should immediately try to catch up with them, and was astonished when the boy objected. Never before had the child rejected Hafed's counsel, and the thought began to rise in Hafed's mind that perhaps Jesus was becoming vain of the gifts that had been so liberally bestowed upon him. However, perceiving what was passing through Hafed's mind, Jesus said, 'Father, I have always been obedient to you, and shown you the reverence which is due to you, and when you leave this world, and your eyes become open to the truth, you shall see why I thus act. Let this for the present suffice you. I am sent to do the work assigned to me, and for this work I must prepare myself so, then, I must obey God rather than man.' Bending before the child, Hafed said he would stay until Jesus was ready to leave.

The next morning, after the ablutions customary in the East, and their morning meal, Hafed and Jesus again went to the temple and there they found assembled the disputants of the previous day. They were ready with fresh arguments to meet him, for he had told them that he would again be there. Many questions were put to him in reference to other countries, and the religious ideas entertained by the peoples of other lands, and astonishing were the replies made by this gifted boy. Bigoted and intolerant as these Hebrews were, they had got their ideas from the right source, but they were unworthy of the privileges conferred on them, and became blind event to the predictions contained in their own books, for when Jesus referred to certain saying of their prophets concerning himself, they did not appear to understand him. He, with great eloquence, also discoursed on the theology of the Egyptians, showing how they had corrupted the truth by their idolatry; and in speaking of Persia and her people, he repelled the idea that they worshipped the sun, and pointed out that it was merely accounted by Persians as the fittest emblem, or symbol, of the Universal Father, who showed his favours on all alike. While thus engaged, his parents, who had come back to the city in search of him, (having only missed him when some distance on their way) entered and chided him for his behaviour to them. He meekly bore their complaints, only saying, 'Know ye not that I must be about my Father's business?' To this they did not appear to pay much attention. Thus turning to Hafed he said, 'Now friend, let us begone.' So it was that they left the city, Hafed travelling a short distance with the holy family, then parting from them to join a merchants' caravan bound for Persia.

Two years later, Hafed received the following letter from Jesus:

'Dear Father Hafed,

I send my greetings unto you. Grace be with you, mercy and peace from God the Father of all. I have many things to write unto you. Since I come home to my people, I often pray for the time that I may meet you once more before I begin my work here. The lands of Egypt and Persia are dear unto me, for there I pass many happy hours in communion with thee and our father the Egyptian.

'Dear Father, when I look around on our people and see how far they have sunk beneath the nations I have visited, in sin and in iniquity, I weary for the time when my labour shall begin; but before that time I shall visit thee again, when we shall travel into the East.

'I send this with a caravan which is about to start for your country. Salute all the brethren that are with you. Grace be with you. Amen.

'Jesus the son of Joseph.'

(The above is in fact a condensed version of the original which contained much that was private between Jesus and Hafed).

# 8

## *Jesus returns to Persia*

During the next few years, through messages received via the spirit of the grove, and seances held within the Magi, Hafed became fully acquainted with many wonderful things Jesus was doing in Israel. When Jesus was eighteen years old, he again sent a letter to Hafed expressing the wish to travel with him in the East, and having received Hafed's promise to do so, he once more arrived in Persia.

By now a tall, fine-looking young man with dark hypnotic eyes and long auburn hair parted in the centre, he was complete in his education. Indeed, Hafed questioned if there was anyone in the whole of the civilised world capable of competing with him. He could speak and teach in a number of languages, and was conversant in many subjects of which very few knew anything, except priests and other learned men.

It so happened that the day Jesus arrived back in the vicinity of the sacred grove was the same day chosen each year in Persia to thank the Great and Bountiful Giver of all good for the gathering in of all the fruits of the earth (Harvest Festival). On that day each year, about the time of the setting sun but before the evening prayers, it was the duty of the Arch Magus to deliver an address suitable to the occasion. However, knowing that Jesus was due to arrive, arrangements were made to welcome him once more. A company of the younger Magi went out to meet him, and he was carried in great triumph with many demonstrations of joy and gladness to the holy hill, where Hafed waited to receive him. However before the Arch Magus had time to express a word of welcome, Jesus raised himself and began to speak to all those who had gathered around him. With marvelous eloquence, and in tones of tenderness and affection, he took up the very subject on which Hafed himself had intended to address the people...the Great Father's love of his children, in crowning the labours of the diligent with his choicest blessings and bounteous crops; and in so doing, drawing their hearts upwards to Himself, the source of all goodness and truth.

Typical of his wisdom, he did not treat the subject of his address from a Jewish point of view, but from the Persian; insomuch that some were heard to say that this was Zoroaster raised again, and teaching better and purer doctrines than ever he had done to the people of old.

With the going down of the sun, Jesus retired to Hafed's cell, there to relate all that had taken place since last they were together in Israel. On entering the cell, with all the simplicity and humility that marked his every action, he flung himself onto the ground at Hafed's feet, and leaning his arms on Hafed's knees, looking up into his face— his countenance beaming with filial love and reverence. Hafed besought him to rise, but no, that was his place he said. At this, the Arch Magus told Jesus that it was more fitting that he (Hafed) should be bending the knee, for had Jesus not just shown that he could outstrip them all, even in the doctrines of Zoroaster. However, firm to his purpose, Jesus said, 'I still love to look on you in reverence. You are one of the few who understand why I am here, and who I am, for there are not many in this world to whom such mysteries have been revealed. But the time will come when the darkness that now covers the earth shall be dispelled by that sun, whose beams shall yet give light to the sons of men. Alas, how sad to see man going down head long in darkness to destruction, with nothing to touch his heart of stone. Instead of being drawn towards Him who sustains them and loves them all with a father's love, men fly from Him as from an enemy. O for the coming of the day when I shall be prepared, my father, to go forth to the work that Thou hast given me to do.'

That night, in the seclusion of Hafed's cell, he and Jesus became witness to many lovely visions, and in the midst of one, they saw again their old friend Issha, the Egyptian priest, clothed in robes of celestial brightness. The form of Hafed's beloved wife, dead for many years past, also appeared before them in all her angelic beauty, as did many other spirits.

# 9

## *Jesus and Arch Magi journey to India*

Two days later, Jesus and Hafed set off on their journey to the East, and being ever in search of knowledge, they made it their business to call at various places of interest on the way, these being chiefly places where communities of Magi were established. It was while travelling through Afghanistan in company with a number of merchants and their attendants, that Jesus once again was to demonstrate his remarkable powers. They were crossing the desert in that country at the time, and the heat being excessive, on coming to a halt, there was great consternation when it was discovered that several of the skins which they thought to be filled with water, were found to be empty; the skins, while the water had been drained off, not collapsing, but retaining their distended shape. The careless servants had thus been deceived, and here they were in the desert without water. The guide of the caravan knew of a spring, but on reaching the place, weary and thirsty, they found it to be dry. Anguish was pictured on every face, for without a speedy water supply, death awaited them. Hafed, in some excitement himself, turned to Jesus and said, 'This is truly a serious matter—what shall we do?'

'Father,' Jesus replied calmly, 'it is good that we should suffer.'

Hafed demurred somewhat to this idea, not seeing the benefit, but Jesus said, 'When we begin to feel the pangs of thirst, with no prospect of water, then it is we feel our weakness; we see the foolishness of placing reliance on man, and are drawn to confide in Him who is ever desirous to bring back the wanderers to trust Him. But have you forgotten the wonderful things that have been done? These can again be done.' Then standing beside the dry spring, he lifted his eyes to heaven and sought help from God, and the answer came as a column of crystal water gushing up from the dry spring into the pure air, and descending in jets of the cool and glorious life-giving element. So much were the weary travellers astonished that forgetting for the moment their burning thirst, they all went down on their knees before Jesus, but he only said, 'Rise and drink.'

In journeying from Afghanistan towards the Plains of Hindustan, they had been compelled to make their way through many difficulties and dangers but, having started in the Autumn, they avoided the burning heat of Summer and also the Winter snows. Having accomplished passage through the famed Bolan Pass in three days, they arrived in what in those days was part of Cashmere. Hafed had in fact visited this area before in his youth (his beloved wife had been a princess of Cashmere) and he had long wished to spend a short time amid its lovely mountains and valleys again.

They visited the Hill Tribes and several of those holy men who had retired from the world in an effort to serve best their Maker. Though not always following the right course, they were at least doing what they thought to be right, and wherever Jesus and Hafed went (as in Persia, Greece, Rome & Judaea) they found men earnestly seeking for spirit-communion, for Divine light and guidance. There were others they met who, setting aside the One Living and True God, the Creator and Sole Sustainer of heaven and earth, believed in many gods. However even they, when pressed by arguments were compelled to admit of the One Great First Cause, and in many cases, once Jesus and Hafed became familiar with them and their ideas, they discovered them nearer to their own way of thinking than they had first given them credit for.

Travelling across the Plains of India, famed everywhere for their beauty, they found well cultivated land and many splendid cities with gilded roofs and towers. They also saw many grand and beautiful temples in their travels, though Hafed frequently remarked that the high and holy One was more readily to be found in a leafy grove than such temples, the works of men. Better to take the wealth lavished on these gorgeous buildings and help the poor and down trodden of the earth's sons.

One place of worship they visited was called 'The Temple of the Elephants'; a vast pile, gorgeously decorated with huge stone elephants supporting a mighty dome, and here they found the people assembled to pay homage to a white elephant. While not condemning the people, Hafed was annoyed that their spiritual leaders should keep the people in such darkness. For size and strength the elephant might be unequalled, but what a miserable object to choose as an emblem of Him, by whose wisdom and power all things were created!

Hafed remarked that in general however, he found the priests of Hindustan to be a very intelligent class and superior to those of Egypt or Persia. They used the pen, were deeply versed in a knowledge of their ancient records, and expounded them. Among them were Sages who from a study of those old records, were looking forward to the coming of a Deliverer of man, and they did not hesitate to open up their books to Jesus and Hafed when it was explained that they wished to gain a knowledge of their theology.

Jesus and Hafed also visited some gorgeous temples of the Brahmins, in which the objects worshipped were ill-shapen, uncouth figures, the work of their own hands, decked out in the richest clothes and jewels of the costliest description; dressed-up blocks of wood to represent their god. Hafed remarked to Jesus how pitiable it was that a people so sincere and so honest in their worship, could sink to such degradation to worship such hideous representations of the Deity as these, and it pained Hafed to stand in what at one time had been accounted the centre of civilisation, the source whence had flown westwards the stream of knowledge, and see these once enlightened people going down into darkness. But then, looking at the young Jesus, he thought, 'here stands one who will yet work a reformation in that system of religion; a religion that was once pure, but the simplicity of which has gone, leaving little but empty forms with deception on one hand and ignorance on the other.' Nevertheless, Hafed (and Jesus) were happy to discover that regardless of the general corrupt state of the religion, there were several temples, especially amongst the Brahmins, where a mode of receiving messages from the spirit world existed, much as existed in Egypt.

After visiting many celebrated temples in various cities and towns, studying the manners and customs of the people as they went, Hafed and Jesus travelled on to the mountainous part of India, where the tops of the mountains were snow-clad all the year round. At length they reached a village (in those days called Zenda), at a very high elevation, near the source of the great river. Here they found one of the finest temples they had yet seen; small, but exceedingly well-proportioned, and connected with the sacred house, a little band of true worshippers.

They learned that the community had been established as a retreat from persecution. They had endeavoured to bring their countrymen to a belief in the truth they held themselves, but had been driven back from the more populous districts to these mountains. They were what some might call hermits. They had their images, but on enquiring, Hafed and Jesus found that these were used merely as symbolic representations. Indeed, Hafed and Jesus thought them the most enlightened priests they had yet encountered, and what with the bracing climate (after the heat of the plains), and the privilege of enjoying such company, they decided to prolong their stay. Hafed and Jesus were even more delighted when they discovered that the Brethren of Zenda received much of their enlightenment through communication with the spirit world, much as the Magi did in Persia. This brotherhood had many ancient writings concerning the theology of their country in bygone ages, and here Jesus attentively studied the Indian theology, and acquired a knowledge of the language.

An object which proved to be of particular interest to Jesus, and especially Hafed, was a large figure carved from a very hard and greenish coloured blood-stone, which stood on a pedestal under the central dome of the temple. It was one of the best figures they had seen in all India and was greatly prized by the priests, who said its weight in gold could not have purchased it. An inscription in hieroglyphic characters ran round the base of the column on which it stood, and there was only one old priest in the community who could read it. Jesus and Hafed were told by him, that therein was contained the whole law and theology of the ancients, with an account of the Creation not unlike that given by Moses.

The brethren assembled at night for their devotions, and Jesus and Hafed frequently joined them. One night when everyone had assembled, and was in a sitting posture around the base of the blood-stone figure, the officiating priest, as usual, went over the service to the Mighty Creator of all things. Each one present, at the close, had uttered the words, 'Abba, Amen!' when just as the last sound had died away in the spacious hall a voice was heard, gentle and sweet, yet so distinct that everyone heard it. The words uttered were, 'Ye men of India who have worshipped me in truth and sincerity, there is one in your midst, even now, who will yet set your poor darkened and deceived brethren at liberty.' Since Hafed and Jesus were the only strangers present, the assembled brethren naturally turned to them, and assumed that since Hafed was the eldest, the voice had referred to him. Realising this, Hafed immediately rose and made known to them everything that he knew concerning his beloved Prince. They would have fallen on their faces to worship him there and then, but Jesus at once checked their intended homage, telling them they must be patient and wait some time yet, for he was but a young man, acquiring knowledge to fit him for the great work that lay before him; but he added that the time would come when the work was to begin, which was destined by the Great Father to give liberty to every prisoner held in the chains of ignorance and sin, in every nation under heaven.

# 10

*Jesus raises dead man in India*

Having remained in Zenda for about two months, Hafed's determination that he should be present at the yearly Festival of the Grove, at last compelled them to leave. On these solemn occasions it was his duty to officiate at the altar, and having missed it one year, he was most anxious to be present at the next. Originally it had been their intention to return via Tartary, but now they had to abandon the idea and take the quickest route...through India to the Arabian Sea, and then by ship to Persia.

On their return journey through India, they rode on camels and elephants, as the came might be. At one place, situated on a branch of the River Ganges, where they stayed overnight, they found on rising with the sun, that a religious service was in progress on the river-bank. Walking to the spot, they observed the dead body of a handsome young man lying in shallow water, while sitting beside him, also in the water, was a young woman, an infant at her breast. The poor young woman sat there, weeping bitterly over the loss of her young husband, whose spirit had not long left him, while friends and relatives sat close by, apparently to prevent her running away. However the poor young creature was so full of grief that in all likelihood she and her child, like the dead body of her husband, would soon become the prey of crocodiles which infested the rivers of India. Although Jesus and Hafed had heard of such a custom, this was the first time they had witnessed the revolting sight. Both stood, looked and pitied, and as they did so they saw the disembodied spirit of the young man floating above his wife and child, earnestly begging them to do something for his little family. Turning to Hafed, Jesus said, 'Father, is not this awful? O for the time when the eyes of this people shall be opened! O that we had men to do the work!' Then turning towards the river again, he exclaimed, 'This time at least, they shall not see this horrible spectacle...this time the monsters shall not find their prey.'

Immediately the waters of the river became very agitated, the crocodiles were seen to rise, but then sink again completely out of sight. Then said Jesus to the distraught young wife, 'Good woman, arise, come to the shore.' At this interference in their usual custom, the friends and relations of the deceased man became very angry indeed and moved towards Jesus to lay hands on him, but he merely turned to look at them and they were stopped as though rooted to the ground, unable to move. By now, the desolate young widow had put one arm around the feet of Jesus as he stood on the bank, her babe cradled in the other, and was looking intently into his face as though in a trance. Then in a calm but commanding voice Jesus said, 'Daughter of the East, arise!' As the woman stood up with her child, Jesus stepped into the water himself and, moving forward, touched the dead body of her husband. Then it was that Hafed, and everyone else present, saw something the like of which their eyes had never before beheld. The spirit, which had been out of the body for some days, drew night, and once more entered the lifeless shell. Immediately, that which had lain like a log of wood in shallow water, rose to its feet, a living man, and walked slowly towards the shore. The people standing on the bank, having recovered from their astonishment, became panic-stricken, and fled in terror. The young widow, seeing that her husband had been restored to life again, moved towards him intending to embrace him, but Jesus quickly perceiving what was her intention (which would have damaged all) called out to her, 'Woman, do it not...wait yet a while.' At length, the young man coming to full consciousness, fell at the feet of Jesus his deliverer, who had no come ashore, and poured forth his soul in gratitude. 'I will now', he exclaimed, 'proclaim thee as the Mighty One. I am of the Brahmin priests, and now that thou hast restored me from death, and in doing this hast given me to see thee as thou art, the son of the Living God, I have a work to do, and I will do it.' Clearly this man, while in his disembodied state, had been able to see the true identity of Jesus, heaven's messenger, and was now led to look upon him as such.

In the years which were to follow, Hafed would learn (through letters sent to him via merchants trading between Persia and the East) that this Brahmin priest was causing a great stir in India. In these letters, he was to tell of the wonderful works done by himself, and the great and unwonted excitement produced on the people by his teachings. He went on to say that the people did not look upon him as a mere man, but as a son of Buddha, adding that when he spoke it was as if he was possessed by Gods, insomuch that the people were at times ready to worship him as a God. This statement clearly showed that the spirit world was making good use of the priest as a medium...a messenger for the furtherance of truth.

# 11

## *The return to Persia*

Having completed their travels in India, Jesus and Hafed set sail for Persia, arriving in the spring, just after the seed-time, which was an every joyous occasion, the birthday of Zoroaster being commemorated at the same time. Their arrival adding interest to the approaching Festival, was manifested in the glad and hearty feeling that animated the brethren when they welcomed them home.

After two days rest, the Festival came on. Everyone was astir early to welcome the glorious orb of day, as he threw out his bright beams on a cold morning sky. The people gathered together and offered up prayers unto him who was represented by the sun, then followed a chant as men, women, and children, all marched in procession towards the place where the Festival was to be held.

After everyone had been seated, and had partaken of a goodly variety of herbs and fruits, washed down with pure water from a nearby fountain, Jesus at length stood up to address the assembly (his last time before returning home to Nazareth), and although he was but a stripling in appearance among these Sages of Persia, all were eager to hear him.

'Men and brethren of Persia. I have spoken unto you on occasions such as this before, and as I am now about to leave you for my own land, suffer me once more to give utterance to my thoughts. men of wisdom and learning and understanding, I thank you for the knowledge you have imparted to me, for all the lessons you have taught me. Here I stand, after travelling with my venerated father amongst nations north and south, east and west. We have searched into their theological systems, into their modes of worship, and their religious practices; but in all our wanderings and searches amongst these peoples, though we have seen much that we considered wrong in their doctrines and worship, and much that was foolish and impure in their religious practices, yet we were oftentimes glad to see traces of great spiritual truths in their ancient books. O men of Persia, servants of the Most High, rejoice that ye are in possession of the light; for alas, many who once had that light now grope in darkness. You proclaim your belief in the One God, the Father of all; He is the True God; all else are false. Brethren, I love you, because of your sincere devotion to truth; I love you, because of your devotion to the welfare of the people; because ye seek not to blindfold the ignorant, but rather to open up to them the fountains of truth and wisdom. My friends and brethren, high and holy is your calling; for to you is committed the education of the youth of Persia; and I love you because ye strive to set before their minds that which will not only benefit them for life on earth, but that which will enrich them in spirit and fit them for heaven. You impart to them all that you yourselves have received in regard to the works of God; and above all, you teach them to live lives of goodness and purity.

'O men of Persia, great and blessed is your work, and precious will be the fruits. But the time draws near when darkness will come upon Persia. Look at that glorious sun... see how he runs on in unclouded beauty. Clouds will obscure his beams for a time, but again he will burst out in blessings over all. These darkened clouds are needed. They play their part in our Great Father's work. Ah, how often, when crossing those sandy deserts, did we long for the dark cloud as a shadow from the scorching heat.

'Brethren, I must leave you to go home to my own land; and there I will, in due time, proclaim to my kindred the truth I am sent to bear unto them. But the day will come when the message, which I must first deliver to my own nation, will be received unto you. Accept O Persians. Farewell, till I meet you in the kingdom where dwelleth the Bright Messenger, from whom ye receive the Heavenly Light. Ah, how often has that high and holy angel dealt with these Jews, my kinsmen, but they have rebelled again and again, and served their own lusts rather than God; they have polluted the holy temple, the house of prayer, and made it a den of robbers. You may think me harsh and unsparing...I can hardly refrain. See me, when but a helpless infant, at my mother's breast, driven into Egypt and finding refuge with one whom these Jews counted an idolater. IDOLATER! Did he bring me up in idolatry?. Well you know how he taught me in truth and light. He, too, is the heavenly country. Have I not seen him...has not Hafed, my reverend father, seen him in all his beauty as an angel? Yes; and he now labours in that work in which he took delight while here on earth, giving light to the blind and unbarring the prison-doors.

'Farewell, my friends. You may forget me for a time, but you will, ere long, hear of me; and the time will yet come when some of you will suffer for me.'

Thus spoke young Jesus, closing with praise and thanksgiving to God. Now that he would shortly be leaving for his homeland, there was a great sadness amongst the Magi, for they had learned so much about the Nazarene—his wonderful works, his spirituality of mind-that they had come to look upon him as something more than man, as one specially endowed by the heavenly powers for the elevation of mankind.

# 12

*Jesus bids Persia and the Magi farewell*

It so happened that about the time of the Festival, the Romans had begun making inroads on the Persian border, thus raising a dispute between the two governments. Since Persia wished to avoid war with the Romans, knowing full well their military might, it was decided that an Embassy of Persian chiefs should speedily be despatched to Rome for some kind of settlement. This, the Magi decided, would be a good opportunity of securing safe conduct for Jesus as far as Jerusalem, through which city the deputation intended to pass.

The night before his departure, Jesus asked the three chief Magi if he might be allowed to visit the main altar in the sacred grove, where he hoped the Spirit of the Flame, the high and holy messenger of God, might yet descend once more. This was granted, and in company with the Arch Magus and other members of the brethren, Jesus went to the sacred grove and stood before the altar, there to wait hopefully for the angelic messenger to appear. The flame from the sacred oil rose brighter and brighter, until finally the flame was quickly dimmed by the appearance of the Shining One, whose effulgence eclipsed even that of the sun at mid-day. The Magi knelt with their heads bent in the dust around the altar, Jesus alone standing up to adore the high and holy God. Turning to the Magi, Jesus said, 'Why thus bend your heads in the dust? Stand erect, and be men. Are ye not noble beings made in the image of God?' At the bidding of Jesus, the Magi therefore all got to their feet, breaking yet one more Persian rule that had stood for centuries. Then the three Magi who had paid homage to him at his birth, came and stood by the side of Jesus directly in front of the altar, and the bright spirit said to them, 'O ye men of Persia, servants of the Great God—ye who were honoured to be chosen Ambassadors of heaven to welcome the birth of the Prince, bearing our gifts to the feet of the holy child—ye who have succoured him and taught him that which he should know, fulfilling your mission to the very letter—look on him now, before he leaves you!'

On turning to obey the instruction of the angel, the three Magi were awe-struck by the sight that met their dazzled eyes...Jesus had become equal in brightness to the Shining One of the Flame. They had seen many times a halo of light around his head, but now the glory of his whole person exceeded all they had every witnessed. The Angel of the Flame bent over him and a voice—but not the voice of the angel—was heard to speak. Each one treasured the sacred utterances, which were never repeated by the, the meanings of which were to remain a mystery till many years later, when Hafed was to meet Paul in the spirit world. Then the first words which Paul addressed to him opened up his mind, and all was clearly revealed.

After this, the spirit took his place in the flame, and all bent their heads in reverence. He thanked them in the name of the Great Spirit for all they had done, then presented them with a small and curiously-shaped casket, which he had taken from beneath the altar where it had lain concealed, and said that the contents were to be devoted to the poor of Persia in return for the services of the Magi to the Chosen One, who was now about to leave them. Hafed opened the casket, and they saw that it was filled with gold coins.

After thanking the bright Angel of the Flame, the Magi engaged in prayer on behalf of Jesus, that he might be shielded from the dangers of the coming journey and, now that his student life was about to close, that he might be directed and strengthened for the great mission on which he had been sent.

Having completed their prayers, they were astonished to see on lifting their heads, the venerable form of Issha, the old Egyptian priest, standing beside the altar, clad in flowing robes of dazzling brightness. As they gazed on the holy visitor with feelings of awe and wonder, the old priest smiled on them and, lifting up his hands, he blessed them, then pointed to a place right beneath the altar of fire, where they saw a small chest. Hafed was directed to open it and, on doing so, saw the precious gold with which it was filled, pour out. He was then told to close it again and hand it to Jesus, who at once said to him, 'Did you ever see this chest before?' At once it flashed to Hafed's memory that he had indeed...when he and Jesus had assembled with the brotherhood of Zenda in their little temple in Northern India...he also remembered that the old priest of Zenda had told him that the chest was to be given to 'One who was to come.' But how came it here, wondered Hafed, and concluded that it must have been aported (brought by spirit-power). Jesus needed money to travel to Judaea, and here it was in abundance, though in truth money was not necessary at all; for Jesus could have travelled by means of spirit-power had he so wished but, except on very rare occasions, he always liked to follow the ordinary way of things.

After the delivery of the chest to Jesus, the Spirit of the Flame (still present) held out his hands towards the three Magi, and as he did so, streams of fire issued forth from his fingers, settling on the heads of each of the Magi in the forms of what appeared to be 'tongues' of fire. Whilst no heat could be felt from this 'fire', it gave to the recipient the ability to receive communications from spirit. This final blessing bestowed, the bright angel once more ascended to the regions of light and love, taking old Issha with him.

Next morning when Jesus had joined the Embassy of chiefs about to depart for Rome, Hafed and a number of the Magi who were loath to part with him, decided to accompany him a short distance and return home before nightfall. However, as the day wore on the brethren decided to remain with the caravan overnight and return home next day so as to have a few extra hours with the beloved youth.

Coming to an oasis, the caravan immediately made camp, and a tent was pitched for the use of Jesus and the brethren. Entering this, they all sat down in a circle, not for the purpose of conversation, but for spiritual communion (a seance). Prayers were said first, the brethren bending their heads low in the dust as was their usual custom, when there burst upon their ears the sound of the most ravishing music, as if all the heavenly choirs had united in one harmonious hymn of praise to the Mighty Creator, while at the same time a most delightful odour pervaded the tent's interior. Lifting their heads in wonder, they were amazed to discover that in fact they were no longer sitting in a tent, but in the midst of a building of immense proportions, lit by thousands upon thousands of lamps, blazing from a lofty dome, like stars, and possessing a brilliance, yet softness which one could not well describe. Around the spacious temple, on seats of gold which were carved with figures beyond the conception of mortal man, sat the glorified spirits of men. The Magi observed that Jesus also had become in appearance like unto these glorious spirits, shining brightly from head to feet. Overcome with awe and wonder, they knelt, not in the dust, but on the golden pavement, and shortly afterwards, on looking up, to their great astonishment they saw that the spirit officiating before the great altar was none other than the old Egyptian priest Issha, and as he laid his offering, as he was wont, on the appointed place, a thousand voices were raised in a harmonious burst of thanksgiving and praise, while ten thousand echoes from the burnished walls of the vast temple sent back the strains upon their ravished ears. Leaving the altar, Issha then came towards the Magi and said, 'You have been favoured more than mortals, for few in bodily form have ever seen what you see now.' He then revealed to them many strange things, all of which appertained to spirit-life. They were also allowed to converse with spirits who had been translated from earth to the spirit-world many generations back. When they were about to leave, Issha said to them, 'This is what you so often desired to see on earth. It is for you a foretaste of that good time, which will yet come to bless mankind.'

Although it seemed like an age they had spent in that blessed place, they had been but the one night in heaven (whether in the body or out of it, they were unable to tell), but when they eventually were transferred back to the earthly plane, the sun had just broken above the horizon and begun his daily course.

After one final prayer to the Great Creator, the Magi in turn all embraced Jesus and parted from him in tears. Hafed was particularly sad, for well he knew he would never see his beloved Jesus in mortal form again, and the glorious youth could not have meant more to him had he been his own son. Jesus did however promise to keep them informed as to his welfare.

# 13

## *John the Baptist*

Even before Christ's birth, Judaea had been a byeword among the surrounding nations for depravity, violence, and murder. Naturally there were a few good men amongst the, and these at certain times in the history of Judaea, shone out like bright stars that twinkled in the heavens. However it was a sad fact that for the most part they were looked down on by their neighbours, and at the time Jesus was to begin his ministry, they had reached the lowest depths of social disorganisation. Terror and distrust reigned everywhere, the occupation of the Roman army, and the treachery and corruption of their own leaders, had conditioned the people to look with eyes of hope upon any man who could present himself as a deliverer from their present sorry state.

To such a nation it was that Jesus's cousin, the prophet and reformer John the Baptist, had been raised to prepare the way for Jesus himself. As had been foretold, even before his birth, John had been fully endowed with the spirit. As he had grown from childhood it became clear that there was something eccentric about him; instruction by ordinary methods was completely lost upon him what he did acquire being ascribed to an inner teaching.

While still a boy, he had exchanged a life of comfort and security at home for a life in the open countryside, his roof the sky, his food wild herbs which he gathered, and his drink water from the wayside streams. His clothing also reflected this nearness to nature, that he refused to wear ordinary garments, and wore instead the skins of animals. Regardless of his strange appearance however, and his eccentric behaviour, John effected great and good work in Judaea, and many were the people of all classes deeply impressed by the truths he so boldly uttered.

He preached to the people in a wild and honest way, the grand truth which our Lord would later elaborate, and truly it can be said that he was a pioneer of Jesus. Nor was his power felt only by the people, Herod the Tetrarch was not ashamed of the company of this wild preacher of the wilderness, but esteemed him greatly, at least for a while.

At this time the Jews generally might be classed under three religious parties or sects: the Pharisees, Sadducees, and Essenes. The Pharisee was known by his strict attention to outward acts of worship, setting himself up as holy and far beyond his neighbours of other sects, because of his conformity to rites and ceremonies, and his long and oft-repeated prayers. He was distinguished from other mortals, as he walked along, by the gravity of his countenance, and the up-turning of his eyes toward heaven...he was hold in his own eyes at least.

The Essenes were men of a very different stamp. From this class chiefly came the followers of the Lord Jesus...being in a manner ready to follow him, because of their similarity to him in doctrine and practice. They were strict in their lives: simple in their habits, eating of the plainest food, drinking no strong drinks, and washing their bodies twice a day, in the cool of the morning and evening. By a strict adherence to this course, many of them lived to a good old age. Their clothing too, was of the simplest kind, insomuch as all they possessed they carried on their backs. None was richer, none was poorer than another. They ate and drank alike, and they were sheltered alike. The children born to them were all equally cared for by the community. Some of these Essenes, like the devout Persians, rose at daybreak and engaged in prayer. On entering a city, they claimed and found shelter from their brethren resident therein. And so, when Jesus and his disciples came into a strange city, it was the poor Essenes of the place who opened their doors to him...not the rich Pharisees, nor the sneering Sadducees.

# 14

## *John baptizes Jesus*

When Jesus returned home from Persia the second time, he immediately renewed his friendship with two of his cousins, James and John (not the Baptist), and soon they became his constant and bosom companions. Indeed the love of John and Jesus was quite remarkable, it was said that where you found one, you could always be sure to find the other; and later still when Jesus began his ministry, and gathered around himself an ever increasing band of followers, whenever they all sat down to rest or eat, it was always John who sat at the right hand of the Master.

Jesus's education by mortal man now complete, he spent more and more time in prayer, deep meditation, and spiritual-communion, this in final preparation for the work he was to do. One day as he was walking near Bethany, on the far side of the Jordan, he came across John the Baptist, and asked that he himself might be baptized, but John was reluctant and said, 'Baptize YOU...it is you who should baptize me.'

'Do as I ask,' replied Jesus, 'for this is as it should be.' John therefore consented, and did as Jesus had bidden him.

After they had stepped from the water, and Jesus had fallen on his knees in prayer, John saw the Spirit of God brightly radiating from Jesus in the form of a Halo round his head, and at the same time a voice was heard to say, 'This is my son, with whom I am well pleased.'

Shortly after this Jesus decided to go into the desert alone for forty days. Fasting for the entire period, he was aware that this, combined with deep prayer and meditation, was the ideal way to bring about a more perfect communication with the spirit-world. At the end of the forty days, when he had become more aware of his own powers and abilities, and the riches those powers could bring him, he was sorely tempted for a moment to change the course he had been sent on. For an instant his hunger tempted him to turn the very stones at his feet into bread, that he might satisfy his hunger, but then the Holy Spirit made him realize that 'man does not live by bread alone—real sustenance comes from God'. Jesus also became aware that his powers could, if he so wished, give him complete control over all the earth, but again the Holy Spirit in the form of Jesus's wisdom, made him realise that such material riches could never bear comparison with anything which the spirit world had to offer. Therefore, casting all temptation firmly aide, he took the course that in his heart of hearts he knew he simply had to take.

## 15

*Water into Wine*

Some time later, the leaders of the Jewish community in Jerusalem, who were becoming increasingly alarmed by the way John the Baptist was continually arousing public opinion against them, decided to send a delegation of priests to question him. 'Tell us,' they asked, and perceiving what was in their minds he replied, 'If you are wondering whether I am the Messiah, the answer is no.' Hearing this, the priests asked, 'Are you then a reincarnation of Elijah?'

Once again John answered 'No.'

'Are you a Prophet?' they asked, and yet again he answered 'No.'

'Tell us then who you are, so that we may report to those who have sent us,' they demanded.

'I am a voice,' he replied, 'just as Isaiah foresaw, I am the voice calling out in the desert PREPARE THE WAY FOR GOD!'

Then asked his questioners, 'If you are not the Messiah, Elijah, or even a Prophet, why are you baptizing people?'

'I do so only with water,' came his reply, 'but there is one standing among you in the crowd who shall baptize with fire, and whose sandals I am not worthy to tie.' Filled with curiosity, but none the wiser, the delegation of priests returned to Jerusalem.

John continued to speak to the large crowd that surrounded him for some time, but later, seeing that Jesus was about to withdraw from his audience, John turned aside and said to two of his disciples sitting close by, 'There goes the Lamb of God—the one who will cleanse the world of sin. He it was I referred to when I said, 'My successor existed before I was born'. He is the son of God, and it is he to whom you should now devote your future attention.' Hearing this, the disciples hurried after Jesus and, as they drew near, he turned to them and asked, 'Why do you follow me?'

'Because our Master, John the Baptist bade us do so,' they replied.

'Then follow me,' said Jesus, and leading them to his lodgings he revealed many things to them.

The following morning, one of the disciples, named Andrew, inspired by all that Jesus had told them, returned home to seek his brother and, on seeing him, he called out in great excitement, 'Simon, we have found the Messiah!' Having listened to Andrew's account of what Jesus had said, Simon too wished to become a follower of his new Master.

Having been introduced to Simon, Jesus said, 'So you are John's son, Simon,' then added 'I am going to give you a new name—Cephas.' (Cephas translated meant Peter, and Peter meant 'Rock').

The following day Jesus decided to go to Galilee, but before doing so, he went in Bethsaida, where he sought out a young man called Phillip. 'Join my band of followers,' said Jesus and Phillip, when he had listened to Jesus speak, was not only eager to follow Jesus himself, but went in search of a friend called Nathaniel, in the hope that he also might follow the Lord. 'Nathaniel,' said he, 'we have found the Messiah—the man Moses and the prophets wrote of. His name is Jesus, and he comes from Nazareth.'

'From Nazareth!' exclaimed Nathaniel, 'Can anything good come from Nazareth?'

'Come and see for yourself,' replied Phillip.

As they approached Jesus, he called out to those surrounding him, 'Now there's an Israelite if ever I saw one—and a man without a trace of deceit in him.'

'How do you known about me?' Nathaniel asked.

'I saw you before Phillip even spoke to you,' Jesus replied. 'I saw you when you were sitting under that fig tree.' (Since everyone's true character is made apparent by the "aura" or spirit-body surrounding the material body, it was a simple matter for a super-psychic such as Christ to make such a deduction).

'You really are God's son' exclaimed Nathaniel, 'and truly Israel's king.'

'You have faith in me because of a little thing like that?' remarked Jesus. 'It is nothing to what you shall see. You are going to see the skies open, and God's holy angels visit me from heaven.'

Two days later, Jesus, his family, and his disciples, attended a Wedding in the town of Cana, some fifteen miles from Nazareth. During the festivities the wine ran out, and Mary, eager for her son to display his supernatural abilities, suggested that Jesus might solve the problem for their hosts. 'Woman,' said he reproachfully, 'that is not our responsibility. My time to act has not yet come in Israel. '

However, feeling sorry for his hosts and their predicament a few moments later, Jesus walked over to where there stood six huge empty stone jars, each capable of holding between twenty to thirty gallons of water, such as was used for the Jewish custom of ceremonial washing. Calling his host's servants, he instructed them to fill the jars with water, and when this had been done, he said, 'Take some to the Master of Ceremonies.' The man having tasted it, turned to the bridegroom and said 'Everybody I know serves his best wine first, bringing out the inferior qualities, when the palates of his guests have become jaded, but you have saved the best until last'.

## 16

### *Jesus displays anger in the temple*

As time passed, Jesus spent more and more time travelling around the countryside, preaching to the people and healing the sick. His band of followers grew in size daily, and when his disciples had come to number seventy, including several of his own brothers, Jesus selected twelve among them to receive special instruction, that at some future date they might serve as messengers to spread abroad his doctrines, though his own family did not number among these more favoured ones.

As the time for Passover drew near, Jesus and his followers went to Jerusalem. There they entered the vast and beautiful temple, and Jesus was appalled to see how desecrated it had become. Its porches were found to be thronged not with devout worshippers, but with persons buying and selling -in short it had become a common market-place.

It was the first time that any of the disciples had ever seen anger on Christ's face, and casting a glance of wrathful indignation on the scene, he drew the cord from around his waist, and twisting it into a lash, with the arm of a giant and the denunciation of a God, he drove out the mercenary herd, turning over their stalls and driving all before him, men and cattle alike, while none dared to withstand him and all fled in dismay. 'Out!' cried Jesus, 'how dare you turn the house of my Father into a market-place.'

After this many of the Hebrews in Jerusalem, of both high and low degree, became followers of Jesus —some secretly. There were also those who were not afraid to speak of him openly, regardless of rousing hostility in both the high priest and Herod, who both wished to crush him. But Jesus was unmoved, quietly saying to those around him, 'Be ye not afraid. My time is not yet come. The work I am sent to do must be finished, and then shall come the time when I am delivered into their hands. '

The disciples however, ignorant of the full meaning of what Jesus declared, thought only how best to gather in more and more adherents, believing that their best strength lay in numbers. Their worst opposition came from the Sadducees—a most abominable sect. The Pharisees—though many of them were thorough hypocrites—had at least some form of piety, but the Sadducees were utterly detestable,—not even being civil to their own households. They had no belief in a future life—their only care being for themselves, quite regardless of the welfare of others. Many a bitter insult they hurled at Jesus and his followers.

How crafty were these Pharisees and Sadducees, thinking that all wisdom and learning was confined to their own little circle...how cunningly they would put their ensnaring questions to Jesus, hoping to trip him and thus enable them to lay some charge against him. They thought him ignorant—a mere carpenter's son. Little did they dream that this simple Nazarene had been educated not only in Egypt, Persia and Rome, but in India and the East. However, regardless of their mean and spiteful opposition, he wearied not in his gracious work for the souls and bodies of the distressed. The plight of the helpless widows and hungry orphans too did not go unnoticed, and whenever his pitying eye caught sight of them, he would turn to the purse-bearer and instruct him to give money to the needy that they might buy food.

In a short time the fame of Jesus had so widely spread around Jerusalem and its neighbourhood, that the people following him wherever he went numbered nearly a thousand persons. Because of this and the problems it presented, Jesus decided to leave Jerusalem accompanied by only the twelve and a few others who included Hermes (an Egyptian who had been a boyhood friend and fellow-pupil under the venerable old Issha). They went from place to place along the shores of Galilee, after which Jesus resolved to send some of those not numbered among the twelve on missions outside of Judaea—some to Rome and Greece, Hermes and others to a town near to Alexandria where a number of devout Hebrews, exiles from Judaea, had erected a synagogue for the worship of God. To these they were to proclaim the truth they had received, telling all that they had seen and heard, and that he whom they had long been waiting for—the Messiah—had come.

The night before departing they all gathered around the supper table, somewhat sorrowful. They felt that with Jesus beside them they were strong, without him, weak. But seeing their sadness of face, he spoke lovingly and wisely to them. He told them not to be disheartened, that though plunged into adversity, made the butt of the scoffer, and denounced as madmen, they had Trust and heaven on their side. Turning to Hermes and two of his companions, Jesus said, 'Show unto my countrymen in Egypt, who have been driven away because of their faith in the promised one, that Messiah has come, and that it is even he who has sent you unto them. Be witnesses for me in all you have seen and heard, and preach to them the great doctrine—love: to do to others that which they would have others do to them. Tell them I love them; I love you; I love all.'

The supper over, those who were to go away bent before him. Then, with uplifted hands he blessed them, asking the Father who sent him to open up their path and strengthen them for the work they were to do. Raising his eyes to heaven, he prayed, 'O glorious and mighty Father, great spirit of all, creator of the worlds, look graciously on these my brethren whom I send forth into the world. O Father, may they know and feel that all strength is to be found in Thee, and that in themselves there is no strength. Give unto them, therefore, that which they lack, that they might be able to declare Thy truth, even unto those who seek their lives, that Thou art indeed their Father and their friend, waiting for their return unto Thee. Great God of truth, may these messengers of Thy truth, sent out to the scattered of Israel, and to the people of the Gentiles, know assuredly that Thou art with them always, and that Thou wilt guide them in the right way, and protect them from all the devices of the wicked.'

After lovingly embracing those who were about to leave, Jesus turned to Hermes and said, ' And thou, companion of my youth; thou who didst share with me the fatherly care and instruction of the good old Issha, I send thee back to thy people and to my people to declare what thou hast seen of me. Go fourth, my brother, strong in the conviction, that God is with thee. I know that thou wilt prosper in the good work set before thee. The holy One in whose service thou art engaged will bless thee; and he who was a father and guide to us when we were boys will, in spirit, still direct thee in thy steps. Look well to thy brethren whom I send with thee. The journey you undertake is beset with dangers, from beasts of prey and men more savage than the beasts. But be not afraid, my brethren, God will shield you from all evil. Beloved, farewell till we meet again. The time will not be long.'

Early next morning, Hermes and his companions left the company of Jesus and his disciples, and began their journey into Egypt.

# 17

## *The man possessed*

Typical of the work done by the followers of Jesus, and the public reaction to such work at the time, is the following story. One day when Hermes and his companions reached the outskirts of a certain village that lay on their route to Egypt, they met a man who was 'possessed' by the spirits of several long-dead people, some good, some bad. One moment he would speak with a voice that was quite angelic, whilst the next moment he used the most profane language imaginable, and the moment Hermes and his companions were entering the village the poor man was being tormented with hooting and howls of laughter from his ignorant neighbours. Hermes and his friends stood for a moment to pity the poor man and, as they did so, the tormented man cried out, 'Behold, there standeth amongst you three men who have just left the presence of the son of God. Hear ye them!'

He had no sooner uttered the words than, possessed by an evil spirit, he broke out in a torrent of bitter curses against Hermes and his companions. Feeling deeply distressed for the man, Hermes commanded the spirits in possession, in the name of Jesus to depart from him. The words were hardly spoken and the man changed from a raging beast to become as quiet as a lamb. His tormentors were amazed and looked first at the man, then at Hermes, but Hermes told the astonished people that there was nothing supernatural in what had just occurred, and that although he might appear to have special powers, these same powers were available to anyone who followed in the foot-steps of Jesus. Then Hermes told them of that God who had led their fathers of old, and whose own son was even now trying to lead them into the paths of truth and holiness.

'Look at this man,' said Hermes. 'He stands now before you in his right mind, and will himself now speak to you.'

The poor man first of all lifted his voice and thanked God, and then turning to the people around him, he told them that henceforth he would devote his entire life to repeating the truths that had just been uttered by those who had set him free. 'I now know that I am a man,' said he, 'Hear I pray you, what these men have yet to tell you; for I have long been lost to myself, and to all that has been going on in Judaea and elsewhere.'

One thing Hermes, in common with all other followers sent on missions, did not realise at the time, was that whenever they performed such feats of goodness, no matter how far away from Judea these might take place, the Master, Jesus, knew fully all that happened...distance did not matter. It frequently caused discussion amongst Jesus's followers, how such a thing could be—did he have information through spirits in sympathy with him and them, or by some magnetic current or chain (Telepathy)? Eventually they were to discover it was the latter, and not only did he use this gift, but when he saw fit, and conditions allowed, he could also effect cures on diseased persons at a distance simply by thought (referred to by 20th century spiritualists as 'distant healing').

# 18

## *The woman at the well*

One day when Jesus and some of the disciples were travelling through Samaria, they arrived on the outskirts of a town called Sychar. It was about noon, they were very weary, and while his companions went off into the town to buy food, Jesus sat down to rest beside a well, known locally as 'Jacob's well' since it was near property once owned by Jacob, the father of Joseph.

As Jesus sat there, a Samaritan woman came to the well to draw water. 'Give me a drink, please,' said Jesus. Knowing that he was Jewish and that the Jews despised all Samaritans, the woman asked, 'How is it that you, a Jew, asks a Samaritan for a drink?'

'If you knew who I am and what God has for you, you would ask me for a drink, and I would have given you living water,' replied Jesus.

Not realising the true meaning of the words he had just uttered, the woman answered, 'You haven't even got a bucket, and this well is deep. Where are you going to get this "living water"? Are you suggesting that you are greater than our forefather Jacob who gave us this well, and drank from it himself, as did all his family and livestock ?'

'Drink of this well-water and you will soon be thirsty again,' said Jesus, ' but anyone who drinks the water I have, will never thirst again. Indeed it shall become as a spring, welling up within, into a life that shall never end.'

'I would like some of that water, sir,' said the woman, 'give me some that I may never thirst again.'

'Go, get your husband,' answered Jesus, and when the woman replied that she did not have one, he remarked, 'That's the truth. You have had five, and the man you are living with now is not your husband.'

Surprised that this stranger should known so much about her, the woman said, 'I see you are a Prophet. Our ancestors have worshipped here on this hillside for generations, but you Jews insist that the only proper place to worship God is in Jerusalem.'

'Listen to me, woman,' said Jesus, 'the time is coming when it will not make the slightest difference where God is worshipped. The time is coming, it is here now, when men will worship God in the way he wants...in their hearts and daily lives. The Father is seeking such people to worship him. God is a spirit, and those who worship him can only do so in spirit and in reality.'

'Oh I know that the Messiah is coming,' said the woman, 'the one they call the Christ, and when he comes he will explain everything.'

Jesus then said to her 'I am he.'

By now the disciples were returning with food from the town, and although they were surprised to see Jesus talking to the woman, they said nothing. As they approached, the woman rushed away in such haste that she forgot all about her water jar. Running into the town-centre she called to everyone she met, 'Come to the well, there is a man there who knew all about my past...I think he is the Messiah!' Soon, quite a large crowd had gathered around her, and together they all set off towards Jacob's well.

Meanwhile, the disciples had been urging Jesus to eat some of the food they had bought, but he did not appear to be hungry, and said to them, 'I have food you do not know about. Listen to me carefully. Do not make the mistake of thinking that the harvest time is in the future. Look about you...the fields are ripe now. The man who reaps now will not only be rewarded for his effort but will be harvesting for the life to come. He and the man who did the planting will celebrate together. That old saying is true: "One man plants, another harvests". You, for instance, are being sent to harvest a crop you did not plant. Others sowed the seed, you receive the benefit.'

By now the crowd from the town had arrived at the well, and some of them who believed what the woman had told them begged Jesus to stay on at the town for a while. He did so for two days. And as a result, many of the townsfolk be came converted.

From Sychar Jesus and his followers went to Cana, and here he was met by a government official from Capernaum who, having learned that Jesus was heading for Galilee, had gone to Cana trying to intercept him. The poor man's son was dying, and he was hoping he could persuade Jesus to return to Capernaum with him.

'You want to see miracles,' said Jesus, 'or you will not believe.'

Desperately anxious for Jesus's help, the man begged, 'Please, sir...come with me. Please, before he dies.'

Moved with pity, Jesus said gently to the man, 'Go home in peace...your son will live.'

Full of trust in Jesus, the man made haste to return home to Capernaum, and with still some distance to go before reach ing the city he met some of his servants on the road, coming to meet him 'He's alive! Your son's alive,' they shouted.

Filled with joy the man asked, 'When did the change for the better begin?' On learning that the improvement had begun the day before, just as Jesus had spoken to him, he jumped down from his horse and fell to his knees, saying a prayer of gratitude to God and showering Jesus with his blessings. From that moment, he and his entire household became followers of Jesus, and great was the welcome they gave him when he finally arrived in Capernaum to preach and teach.

## 19

*Jesus gathers more disciples*

The sabbath came, and Jesus taught in the synagogue. His words range with authority and he made a deep impact on the congregation, but in the midst of the service there was a great commotion when a man who had ben sitting quietly, suddenly leapt to his feet and possessed by an evil spirit shouted out, 'What have we to do with you, Jesus of Nazareth? We know you, you are God's holy one. Have you come here to destroy us?'

'Quiet!' commanded Jesus. ' Come out of him!' The man went into a series of convulsions, then giving a loud shriek of protest, the evil spirit departed from him.

Great was the consternation in the synagogue, with everyone asking his neighbour, 'Whatever is going on?...What is this, some new religion?...Did you see the way this new preacher handled the man...what control he has—even over devils!'

When the service was over, Jesus was invited to the home of two friends, Simon and Andrew. The disciples James and John had been invited also. When they arrived, they found that Simon's mother-in-law was burning with a fever. Jesus was taken to her bedside, and as he took her hand and raised her, so her fever left her and she got up and prepared the food for her son-in-law's guests.

That evening, just before the setting of the sun, a crowd gathered outside the house, for word of Jesus's powers had quickly spread, and it seemed the whole town was there; anyone who had sick relatives or friends had brought them to the house. Going out and walking amongst them, Jesus put forth his hands, healing those who were sick in body, and driving out evil from those who were possessed. Some, recognizing who he truly was, shrieked at him, 'You are God's son!' These he ordered to be silent.

Next morning Jesus went for a walk along the shore of the lake, and in a very short spaces of time a crowd had formed, and was following him. As he continued to walk, he noticed two boats pulled up on the shore, and the men who owned them were standing in the water washing their nets. Seeing that one of them was Simon, his host the previous evening, Jesus stepped into his boat and asked that Simon push it into the water, so that he might sit in it and talk to the crowd gathered along the shore.

When he had completed his teaching, Jesus wished to repay Simon for allowing him use of his boat, and so turning to Simon he said, 'Put out to where the water is deeper and cast your nets.'

Simon answered saying, 'But we have been fishing all night, Sir, and have caught nothing...however, if you say so, then we will try again.'

Having rowed some distance from the shore, Simon and his friend, Andrew, cast their nets and when the two men began hauling them in again, they found to their dismay that they had encompassed a school of fish so large that the weight of their catch had begun to rip the nets. Frantically they waved to their partners John and James, standing on the shore, and called out to them to bring the other boat. When finally all the fish had been landed, both boats were so heavily laden that they were in danger of foundering.

Suddenly, waking to the realisation that his good-fortune had come about as a result of Jesus's powers, Simon fell at the feet of the Master, saying, 'I am not worthy. I am too wicked a man to follow thee.'

Raising a hand to silence him, Jesus said, 'Do not worry Simon...in the future you shall be a fisher of men.'

When the boats had been beached, Jesus turned to Simon and Andrew saying, 'Come and join me,' and leaving everything...their boats, nets, tackle and fish, they followed him.

James and John had by now rejoined their father, Zebedee, and were repairing their nets, but when Jesus also called out to them, 'Come and join me,' then they also turned their backs on everything and followed him.

Jesus travelled all over Galilee, and eventually he returned home to Nazareth. Here, on the sabbath, as was his custom, he went to the synagogue, and standing up in the congregation to read, he was handed the scroll of the book of Isaiah. Unrolling it until he found the portion he sought, he read...

'God's spirit rest upon me.
He has anointed me to tell the good news to the poor.
He has sent me to announce liberty to the prisoners,
To the blind, the restoration of their sight,
To the oppressed, freedom from their bonds,
And to proclaim the day of grace God has set.'

Having read, Jesus rolled up the scroll, handed to an attendant and sat down. Then with all eyes upon him he said, ' Today, here in your presence, that prediction has been fulfilled.'

However, apart from healing a few who were sick, he was able to accomplish little, so great was the disbelief that filled most of them. 'How does he come by his powers?' they asked each other, 'How does he do these things?...isn't he the son of Joseph the Carpenter? We know his mother, brothers and sisters. Where does he get such notions?'

Soon, their criticism and indignation had developed into anger at what they considered to be his arrogance. Sensing their hostility, Jesus said to them, 'I suppose you are going to quote to me the old proverb, "Doctor, heal thyself"..."show us here those miracles they say you performed in Capernaum". How true it is that a prophet shall be honoured everywhere except in his own home-town, and by all except his own friends and relations. Let me refresh your memories,' he continued. 'Back in the time of Elijah—the time when there was a great drought and it did not rain for three and a half years, resulting in a great famine, and there were many widows in Israel. Was Elijah sent to help the Israelites? No, he was sent to a widow who lived in Zarapath in Sidon...a Gentile. Also, back in Elisha's time there were many Lepers in Israel...but did Elisha heal any of them? No, the only leper he healed was Naaman, and he was a Syrian.'

By now, enraged by his words, the people seized Jesus and dragged him out of the synagogue. Through the town they marched him, to the brow of the hill on which Nazareth stood, and here they would have thrown him over the rocky edge, had he not managed to escape from their hands and vanish.

A few days later he returned to Capernaum. Word quickly spread that he was back, and in a very short time people were flocking to the house where he was staying. So eager were they to see and to hear him, that they not only filled the house, but overflowed out into the courtyard as well.

Among those so eager to reach Jesus, were four men carrying another man on his sleeping-mat...he was paralyzed with the palsy. Seeing how dense was the crowd outside, the four men climbed on to the roof of the house, carrying the poor man up with them. Then, making a large hole in the roof, they lowered the man down into the room where Jesus was teaching. Seeing what an act of faith these men had performed, Jesus spoke to the sick man, saying, 'Be of good cheer my son—thy sins are forgiven thee.'

Now among the people crowded into the room, were some Pharisees and teachers of the law, and they spoke to each other with indignation, saying, ' This is blasphemy. Who does this man think he is that he can forgive sins? No one but God can do this.'

Hearing their remarks, Jesus asked, 'Why are your thoughts so evil? I put this question to you; which is the easier, to tell a man that his sins have been forgiven, or tell a man with the palsy to get up, pick up his bed and depart? I ask you, which is the easier? And now, to make it clear unto you that the son of man is authorized here on earth to forgive sins...' He turned to the man stricken with the palsy and said, 'Get up; pick up thy bed and return home.' Immediately the man got to his feet, rolled up his mattress and left the house, shouting praises to

Almighty God as he went, whilst the people crowded into the room all stared in astonishment, and excitedly chattered about this great act of healing which they had just been privileged to witness.

When Jesus left the house, the crowd continued to follow him, so entranced were they, and having made his way down to the Lake, he proceeded to teach for a little longer. Later, walking through the streets of the city, he chanced to meet a tax-collector named Levi, sitting at his toll-booth. 'Come—join me,' Jesus said, and obediently Levi (later called Matthew) rose, and leaving everything behind him proceeded to follow Jesus.

That night Matthew gave a feast, to which he invited Jesus, the disciples, and a number of the less reputable citizens of Capernaum. Some Pharisees, aware that Jesus had gone to this particular feast, were outraged. 'Why does your Master associate with such rabble?' they enquired of the disciples. When later the question was repeated to Jesus himself, he replied, 'It is the sick who need a doctor...not the healthy. God prefers acts of mercy to sacrifices in the temple. I am not come to instruct the righteous, but to call the sinners to repent.'

At another time the disciples of John the Baptist came to Jesus, and said, 'Why do we and the Pharisees observe the days of fasting, but your disciples do not?' Jesus answered saying, 'Should wedding guests be mournful when the bridegroom is still with them? The time for fasting is when the bridegroom has left them.'

Always fond of using parables, Jesus also said, 'No one mends a hole in an old garment with a piece of unshrunken material, for when the patch shrinks, it would tear the cloth around it.' And another time: 'Men do not store new wine in old wineskins, for the skins would burst and the wine be wasted. Instead they put new wine in new wineskins, so that both may be preserved.'

# 20

## *Jesus angers officials*

One day a certain important official, having heard about the healing-powers of Jesus, came from a neighbour city and implored him to come and lay hands on his beloved daughter, saying, 'Sir, I know she is very near to death, but I know that if only you will put your hands upon her, she will live.'

Arriving at the official's home, it was found that relatives and friends were already wailing and mourning the little girl. However Jesus spoke to them saying, 'Cease your mourning, for the child is not dead, she merely sleeps.' Hearing this, the mourners laughed scornfully at him, thinking and saying amongst themselves that he must indeed be mad. But when Jesus had been led into the room in which the child lay, and he had taken her hands into his own, her spirit which had not yet fully withdrawn from her, returned to occupy her once more, and she rose from her bed completely restored. Those who only moments before had been so scornful, were now filled with dismay and wonder, and quickly the news of yet another 'miracle' spread for miles around.

It was also about this same time that yet another great act of healing was demonstrated to many people. At the time, Jesus had been preaching to a large crowd around him, and having completed his message for them, he was about to leave and was making his way through the throng who pressed in on him from all sides, when suddenly he stopped, and said loudly, 'Who has just touched me?' Since so many people were pressing against them, his surrounding disciples thought this an odd question to ask; however Jesus persisted and asked 'Who touched me?' It was then that a poor woman in the crowd, who had been slowly dying of cancer for the past twelve years, spoke out and said, 'Forgive me Master, it was I—but I felt that if only I could get near enough to touch you, then I would be cured.' Deeply moved by the woman's faith in him and his abilities, Jesus said to her, 'Daughter, be comforted, for this day thy faith hath restored thee to full health,' and immediately the woman was made whole again.

Many were the acts of healing which Jesus performed at that time, the blind were made to see, the deaf to hear, the dumb to speak, and those who were insane had their 'devils' driven out of them. Wherever he went, teaching in the synagogues or preaching in the towns and countryside, Christ would be filled with compassion for the unfortunates he saw everywhere around him.

One day when Jesus had gone to Jerusalem to observe one of the Jewish festivals, he visited a well known pool called Bethesda. Surrounding the pool were five porches, and in these sat large numbers of people with a variety of ailments, waiting for the 'movement of the water'. It was said that at certain seasons an angel descended from heaven to disturb the water, and whosoever was the first person to enter the pool after the waters had been stirred was immediately cured of whatever disease or ailment he might have.

Sitting by the edge of the pool was a certain man who had suffered a lingering infirmity for the past thirty-eight years. Seeing him, Jesus went up to him and said, 'Wilt thou be made whole?' The man replied that this was his dearest wish, but added, 'Sir, I have no one to lower me into the pool, and whilst I am attempting to descend into the water there are always others more nimble than I, who are able to take advantage.'

Pitying the poor man's dilemma, Jesus said to him, 'Rise, take up thy bed and walk.' Immediately the man rose to his feet, and to the astonishment of all those around, proceeded to roll up his bed and walk away. As he was about to depart however, a group of Jewish officials said to the man, 'This is the sabbath-day, and it is not lawful for you to be carrying your bed-roll.' The man answered, 'He that healed me said, "take up thy bed and walk".' Hearing this, the officials at once requested that the healed man point out to them the healer who had spoken to him th us. However, since Jesus had wished to avoid drawing further attention to himself, he had slipped quietly away.

Later, when visiting the temple, Jesus chanced to meet the man from the Pool of Bethesda again, and said to him, 'Thou hast been made whole, but make sure you sin no more, or next time you will fare worse.'

By now, the temple officials had discovered that it was Jesus who had been responsible for the man's remarkable recovery, and when they had sought him out, they asked him why it was that he had performed such work on the sabbath-day, and Jesus had replied, 'My Father knows no distinction in the days, and no more do I.'

This statement infuriated the officials, for not only had he broken sabbath law, he actually (in their eyes) had the audacity to claim he was equal with God! This they decided was really too much and they were determined not simply to bring about his downfall, but to seek his execution.

Facing them on the question of his status with God, Jesus said, ' The truth is, I do nothing of my own choice...I simply follow my Father's example. He loves me, and has disclosed his purpose to me. He is going to reveal even more astonishing things to me yet, so be prepared. It is the Father as you know who raises the dead, so also do I, his son, give life to whomsoever I please. God no longer judges mankind, this he has now put entirely into mine own hands, so that I may be honoured equally with him. If you fail to honour the son, then so too do you fail to honour the Father than sent him.

'Anyone who heeds what I say, and believes in the God that sent me, shall have eternal life. And because he shall have passed from death to life, he will not face the judgment. The time is coming, indeed it is here now, when those who have been as "dead" all their lives shall hear my voice, and hearing (awakening) they shall live forever. The Father (the Great Spirit) is the essence of life, and I have been endowed with the authority, as the son of man, to be the judge of all mankind. The time is coming when, as I have already said, the spiritually dead will hear my voice and come out of their graves of ignorance. Those who advance in spiritual growth and understanding shall live forever in light and glory, while those who close their ears to me, and spend their earthly lives concerned solely with material benefits and sins of the flesh, and have committed evil, shall be condemned. The authority I exercise is not my own; I judge as God bids me, and because of this my judgments are fair, for I am not expressing my own will but the Father's. I can of my own accord do nothing; As I hear, I judge, and my judgment is just, because I seek not to impose my own will, but the will of the Father who has sent me.

'I do not ask that you accept what I have said out of hand, and without authentication...this you have had in plenty; not only did the prophets of old foretell of my coming, but more recently John the Baptist hath spoken of me, and indeed prepared the pathway for me. He was a bright and shining light, and you were, for a while, happy to bathe in the warmth of that light, but there is confirmation far greater than anything John could offer; namely those things which God has empowered me to do, things I have already demonstrated, they are the proof that the Father has sent me...He is my witness. His voice speaks to you through me, but you refuse to listen—rather would you devote yourselves to the Scriptures, in the belief that these will lead you into everlasting life. Those same Scriptures speak of me, but you are so blinded by doctrine that you refuse to see that I am the donor to that eternal life.

'I seek not praise from you nor any man, but it is clear that there is no real love for God in your hearts, for though I come with full authority of the Father, you have spurned me. Yet let some lesser person come offering nothing more than himself, and you will accept him with open arms.

'How can you call yourselves believers? You refuse honours which come from the one and only God, yet accept honours from other mortals like unto yourselves.

'Do not think I accuse you before the Father—Moses has already done that! For had you believed Moses, you would have believed me, but if you refused to believe his writings, is it any wonder that you do not believe my words?'

Some time later, on yet another sabbath-day, Jesus was again to offend the over-sensitive Pharisees. It came about because he and some of the disciples, walking through a wheat field on their way to a synagogue, plucked some grain, and having rubbed it between the palms of their hands to be rid of the chaff, then ate the kernels.

A group of Pharisees seeing the incident, immediately seized the opportunity to complain about the behaviour of the disciples. Going up to Jesus they asked, 'Why do you allow your disciples to break the sabbath laws this way?'

Jesus replied, 'Have you not read in our History—about the time Abiathar was high priest, how king David and his men, because they were famished, went right into the temple and ate the presentation loaves, a thing which only a priest was permitted to do? And have you not read that in the law, priests are permitted to work on the sabbath without breaking the law? What I do is far more important than what is done in the temple, and you would realise this if you had any understanding of the Scripture—*I prefer acts of mercy over the offering of sacrifices in the temple.* The sabbath was established to benefit mankind—not the other way about.' So saying, Jesus and his followers continued on their way to the synagogue.

Among the people attending this particular synagogue that day, there chanced to be a man with a withered hand, and the Pharisees, now ever-eager to bring complaints against Jesus, wondered if he would attempt to heal the man. When in fact Jesus did summon the man to be healed, the Pharisees quickly spoke up saying, 'Is it lawful to heal on a sabbath day?'

Jesus answered them, 'Who among you if a shepherd, finding that one of your sheep had fallen into a pit, would not attempt to pull it out on a sabbath day? Is not a man's worth greater than a sheep and where does it say that one shall not do good on sabbath days?' Then said Jesus to the afflicted man, 'Stretch forth thy hand that Almighty God might heal thee,' and instantly the man's hand was completely restored.

Full of anger and evil thoughts, the Pharisees left the synagogue and held a meeting, to discuss how best to deal with Jesus and destroy him, but being informed of their intentions, Jesus and his followers withdrew to safety in Galilee. Now, because the Jews were proving themselves to be such an unworthy people (as so often in the past), Jesus determined to give more and more of himself to the Gentiles.

# 21

### *Jesus condemns scribes and Pharisees*

In Galilee, once again because of his growing fame, the people flocked to hear him speak and receive healing. One day there was brought to him a man possessed of an evil spirit, who was also blind and dumb. Filled with compassion as always, Jesus healed the man, and everyone (except the Pharisees) marvelled that the man was able to see and to speak again. The Pharisees merely remarked, 'This man Jesus is in league with Satan, and it is from him that he draws his powers.'

Hearing what they said, Jesus replied, 'Every kingdom that is divided against itself, perishes. Likewise every city or home that is divided against itself, must also perish; if Satan casts out Satan, is he then not divided against himself? And how shall his kingdom stand? If I am able to drive out evil spirits because I am in league with Beelzebub, as you say, with whom are your priests in league when they drive them out? If however I expel them through God's Holy Spirit, does it not surely mean that God's kingdom has arrived through me, thought you refuse to believe it. Likewise, you must be aware that anyone wishing to break in and plunder the house of a strong man must first overpower the strong man himself. He that is not with me is against me, and those who do not help me in gathering adherents are in fact scattering God's flock.

'Let me draw especially to your attention that although all manner of sin and blasphemy shall be forgiven man, not so blasphemy against God's Holy Spirit. You may blaspheme against me and be forgiven, but never against Almighty God...that shall be an eternal sin. Either be as a good tree bearing good fruit, or as a corrupt tree bearing corrupt fruit, for the tree shall be known by the fruit it bears.

'You generation of vipers. Being evil, how can you spread good? good can flow only from the good, just as evil always exudes from the wicked. But I tell you now, every evil word that men speak, just as every evil deed they do, shall be accounted for.'

Then some among the scribes and Pharisees called out, 'Master, give us some proof of all that you say.'

'Only such an evil and adulterous people such as you would ask for proof!' retorted Jesus, 'but none shall I give thee, except to say that as Jonah was three days and nights in the belly of a whale, so in time shall I be three days and nights in the heart of the earth.

'On judgment day, the citizens of Nineveh will stand up in condemnation of this generation, because they repented when Jonah preached—unlike you who have an even greater one than Jonah come amongst you!

'On judgment day the Queen of Sheba too shall stand in condemnation of this generation, for she travelled great distances to listen to the wisdom of king Solomon. And look, you have among you someone even greater than Solomon.

'When a sinful man has died, and his spirit has left his earthly shell and arrived in the spirit world, he shall find that he has been allotted only dark and desolate places in which to wander, and since like always attracts like unto itself, he shall find himself surrounded by spirits all equally evil, and they shall between them each create their own "hell". Thus shall it be with all your wicked generation.'

Here Jesus paused for a moment, and as he did so, a good woman in the crowd who had been listening to all that he had said, called out, 'Happy the womb which brought thee forth, and the breasts which gave thee nourishment!' Jesus answered saying, 'Happier still those who hear God's word and obey him.'

While Jesus had thus been speaking to those assembled in the synagogue, his mother and his brothers arrived and wished to speak with him. However, so eager was the crowd to hear Jesus speak that they were unable to get into the building.

When word was passed to Jesus that his mother and brothers awaited without to speak to him, he only answered, 'Who is my mother and who is my brother?' Then stretching forth his hand towards his disciples, he said, 'Behold, there are my mother and brothers. For whosoever shall do the will of my Father in heaven, the same is also my brother, sister and mother.'

## 22

### *Jesus teaches with parables*

A few days later when Jesus left his house to walk by the sea-shore, the crowds which followed him were so large that to save himself from being crushed, he climbed into a small boat and sat a little off-shore to speak to the people in a series of parables.

'Here is a man sowing seed,' he said 'Some of it falls on the road, some is trampled into the dust by passers-by, and birds eat the rest. Some seeds fall on a gravel patch. It sprouts quickly, but it withers and dies in the scorching heat of the sun because it is not deeply rooted. Some of the seed falls among weeds. It grows, but the weeds grow even faster and choke it. Some seed falls on good fertile soil, and this gives a great yield; from thirty to a hundred times the amount sown.' Then said Jesus to the people around him, 'If you have ears to listen with, then hear the call.'

Later the disciples asked Jesus, 'Why do you so often speak in parables to the people?' He answered saying 'You have been permitted some understanding of the mysteries of God's kingdom (Creation), but not so others. Those who already have some understanding shall be given even more, but those who lack understanding shall receive nothing, and remain barren. I use parables to puzzle my enemies; they may think they get the proper meaning behind the stories, but they do not. Such men are typical of those whom Isaiah prophesied, saying "Hear they may, but understand—never". For their hearts have grown hard, their hearing has become dull, and their eyes have become clouded. Only when they really open themselves up to God shall a full understanding be granted to them.'

Then said Jesus to the disciples, 'You have been blessed, for your eyes and ears have revealed the real truth to you. Many are the prophets and godly men who have longed to see what you have seen, and hear what you have heard, but never were they given the chance.

'Now, regarding the parable just told; if you have been unable to grasp its meaning, how shall you understand those to follow? The seed represents God's word, and the seed that fell on the road can be compared with people who hear the word, but have it snatched from them by evil ones before they can accept it and be saved. The seed that fell on the gravel patch is like unto those who on hearing the word, eagerly and happily accept it, but who, because they are shallow, cannot endure temptation, trouble, or persecution and fade quickly away. The seed that fell among the weeds, is like unto people who hear the word, but through the difficulties of everyday life, and their pre-occupation with material things, allow their good intentions to slip away from them. The seed sown in fertile soil however, is like unto those who, hearing and understanding the word, work patiently to produce a bountiful harvest...from thirty to one hundred times more than that which was sown. No one,' Jesus continued, 'lights a lamp only to hide it under a bed—you put it on the table where it can lighten the whole room. Nor do I hide any secrets from you. If you have ears, listen, and make sure to pay careful attention, for the care with which you listen will determine how much knowledge and understanding shall be bestowed upon you.'

Then teaching through even more parables he said, 'The Kingdom of Heaven is like unto a man who plants some seed which, when it grows, develops from first a tiny shoot, to a full-grown plant. He does not understand how it all happens, but that does not stop him harvesting his crop when it has become ripe.

'Again, you may consider the Kingdom of Heaven in the following way; A man sows a field of wheat, and under the cover of darkness an enemy scatters the seed of weeds on the same soil. Both the wheat and the seeds flourish. The man's servants ask if they should pull up the weeds but their master replies, "No, for in doing so you may also uproot the wheat.

We will wait until harvest time, and then we will pull up the weeds and burn them. Then we will gather in the wheat and store it" .'

Continuing, Jesus said, 'You may also compare the Kingdom of Heaven to a mustard seed. Though one of the smallest of all seeds, when fully grown, it is large enough to accommodate birds seeking shelter in its branches.'

'Yet again, you might also compare the kingdom to the making of bread. A woman takes a little yeast, and having added three measures of flour, soon the yeast has permeated all of it.'

At last Jesus withdrew from the crowd, and went into the house where he was staying, followed by the disciples. However, once inside, a disciple said, 'Master, explain to us the parable of the wheat and the weeds.'

When everyone was therefore seated comfortably, Jesus once more began to teach. 'The field is the world,' he explained, 'the good seed like the children of heaven, whilst the weeds are the weeds are the children of evil. The enemy that sowed them is the Devil, and the harvest is the end of this earthly life. At the end of their earthly lives, all the people who have committed evil during their lifetime shall be cast into an environment of spiritual torment, compatible with their evil characters. Thus will they find themselves transported into a hell of their own making, and there shall they remain until such time as they have fully repented. The righteous however (the good seed), shall be gathered up at death and be transported to a spiritual world of light, joy, and eternal blessings (heaven).

'Liken also, the Kingdom of Heaven unto the man, who, having found a great treasure hidden in a field, goes out and sells all his possessions in order to buy that field, and so obtain the treasure. Or it is like a man who has found a pearl of great value, and likewise sold all his possessions in order to obtain it. Better still, compare it to the fisherman who, having cast his net into the waters and gathered in fish of every kind, pulls the net into the boat, keeps all those fish which are good and throws back all those which are bad. So shall it be at the end of each person' s life.'

And when he asked them if they had understood his teachings, they answered 'Yes Lord.'

# 23

*The Baptist beheaded: Feeding the 5,000*

Throughout these early years of Christ's ministry, his cousin John the Baptist still continued to expound the truth of God in his own inimitable way, but the day came when John dared to criticize the unlawful union of King Herod and his sister-in-law, Herodias (the king's own wife having fled to her father for protection). Herodias, incensed with bitter hatred at what she considered to be John's audacity, was determined to seek revenge. To appease her anger, Herod had John arrested and thrown into prison, but this did little to stem the loathing which Herodias now felt for him, and she made up her mind that one way or another, she would bring about his death.

Her opportunity came a short time later, when plans were being made at the palace to celebrate the king's birthday. Knowing that Herod was particularly attracted to her daughter Salome, Herodias arranged for the girl to perform a very seductive dance as a highlight to the evening's festivities. So entranced was the king by the girl's dancing that there and then, before all his assembled guests and courtiers, he asked the girl what she desired as a reward, and swore that she might have anything she chose. Having been previously instructed by her mother, the girl immediately replied, ' The head of John the Baptist on a platter!'

The King, and indeed the whole Court were horrified, but knowing that he had sworn a public oath, Herod had no alternative but to grant the girl her grisly request and, calling for his guards, he instructed them to carry out the order.

Having admired the Baptist so much in his earlier days, Herod regretted deeply the step he had been tricked into taking, and never more was he to prosper; in later years he would be removed from his kingly office by the Roman Government, who were then to banish him, while the wretched Herodias would have to flee to distant Spain as a fugitive.

News of the foul deed, quickly spread far and near, and everywhere the people were appalled. John's disciples having collected the body, immediately buried it.

When the news reached Jesus, he decided to go to a quiet area of countryside near Bathsaida, there to meditate with his own disciples. However, large numbers of people, distressed and seeking consolation from Jesus and seeing him depart by boat, hurried along the shore in the direction which he was going, in fact arriving in time to greet him as he stepped ashore.

Feeling great compassion for the masses, as always, Jesus immediately healed many who were sick, and then began to preach to them. Time passed, and as the sun began to set, one of his followers said to Jesus, 'Master, the hour grows late, and the people grow hungry, should we not send them into the town to buy food for themselves?'

Jesus replied, 'That is not necessary; give them something to eat.' Then as a test of faith, he turned to Philip and asked, 'Where can we buy food, Philip?'

Surprised, the disciple answered, 'Master, a year's wages would not buy sufficient food for all the people assembled here this day.'

Calmly Jesus said, 'How much food have we ourselves?'.

Andrew answered, 'None at all. There is however a boy here with five barley loaves and two fishes, but what good are they with so many to feed? There must be at least four or five thousand people here!'

'Bring me the loaves and the fishes,' said Jesus, 'and have the people sit on the grass in groups of fifties or hundreds.' Then taking the food in his hands, he first blessed it, then broke it into small pieces, passing it to the disciples for distribution to the multitudes. Incredibly, the supply of food passing from his hands to the disciples continued until all the people sitting on the hillside had eaten enough and were satisfied. Then Jesus said to his followers, 'Gather up the fragments of food which remain,' and to their utter amazement they discovered that there was enough to fill twelve large baskets.

Their hunger now satisfied, Jesus dismissed the people and told them to return to their homes. Then he bade his disciples return to Capernaum in the boat and, alone he climbed a nearby mountain where he wished to pray and meditate in the darkness.

Some hours later as the disciples were sailing towards Capernaum, a violent storm broke out and the huge waves which quickly developed, threatened to overturn their small craft. They remembered being caught in a similar situation only a few weeks previously, but on that occasion Jesus had himself been with them, sleeping peacefully, his head on a cushion. In fear lest any moment the boat should capsize, they had woken their Master, and he had said to them, 'Why are you afraid? Have you not yet learned to have trust in the Lord?' Then standing up in the boat he had raised his hands towards heaven and said 'Peace...be still,' and immediately the winds had stopped their raging, and the sea had become calm, causing the disciples to marvel at their Master's control over the forces of nature. Now however, faced with identical conditions they were alone, and fearful of what would happen to them.

But high on the mountainside, as he knelt in deep meditation, the telepathic communications which always subconsciously transmitted themselves between his followers and himself, made him aware of their immediate difficulties and, rising to his feet, he at once spiritually transported himself to the area where they were struggling to stay afloat.

His sudden appearance, walking on the surface of the sea, was a great shock to them and at first they were unable to believe what they were seeing, imagining it to be some kind of hallucination. However, the next moment he called to them saying, 'Fear not, it is I.'

Then Peter called out, 'Master, if it truly be you, allow me also to come across the surface of the water to thee.'

'Come then,' replied Jesus, and Peter climbed over the side of the boat and commenced to walk towards Jesus. Having gone but a short distance however, his courage and his faith suddenly deserted him and, unable to maintain his psychic state of exaltation, he began to sink down into the water, calling out, 'Save me, Master!' as he did so.

Immediately Jesus reached out and grabbed hold of him, saying, 'How little faith you have, Peter—you should have trusted me.' Together now, Jesus and Peter then walked across the surface of the water to the boat, and as they climbed aboard, so the winds dropped and the sea became calm. The disciples were astounded. They had failed earlier to grasp the significance of the 'miracle' of the loaves and the fishes, but now suddenly, all became clear to them, and they fell at their Master's feet saying 'Indeed you are the son of God.'

The storm having now subsided, they made their way to Gennesaret, and here they beached the boat. It was now morning, and as Jesus stepped ashore, he was instantly recognized by some people who quickly spread the news that he had landed, and all those with sick relatives hurriedly brought them down to the shore that Jesus might cure them. One man in the crowd called out, 'We need only to touch the hem of your robe,' and all those who did so were in fact healed.

On the other side of the lake, some of the people who the previous day who had been miraculously fed with the five loaves and the two fishes, came by boat searching along the shore for him. Eventually they found him in a synagogue at Capernaum. Knowing their motives for seeking him, Jesus said unto them, 'You have not come here because you hunger for the truth, only because you hunger in your stomaches. Waste not your time in a quest for perishable foods, but search instead for the food that lasts for ever.'

'Tell us what God requires of us,' asked one man.

Jesus replied, 'That you believe in him who has been sent to you.'

'We will believe if only you offer us the kind of proof Moses gave to our ancestors in the desert, when he gave them manna to eat,' the man said, 'not only was the manna a sign from God, it also fulfilled the prophecy: *"he will give them heaven's bread to eat".*'

'Moses did not produce the manna,' said Jesus, 'my Father did; the same one who now offers you the real "heaven's bread" (the truth) that has come from heaven to feed the world. I am the bread, partake of me and you will never go hungry, trust me and you shall never thirst. I offer you abundant proof in so many ways, yet still you refuse to believe in me.

'I am here to do God's will, not my own. It is his will that I raise to a greater level of understanding and awareness all those who will trust in me, so that on the day they leave their earthly bodies, and leave their spirit free to enter the world of spirit, they shall become fully aware of the eternal existence they face in one sphere or another. '

Some of the crowd, unable to comprehend what Jesus was saying, muttered to each other, 'What is he talking about, and what does he mean, saying that he is heaven's bread?'

Then said Jesus to them, 'Only those who really believe in God will come unto me, and only those who believe in me, will live for ever in true understanding. I am the bread of eternal life. Your ancestors ate the food of earth and died; I offer you the food of heaven, that you might live in knowledge for ever.'

Many people in the crowd now began to argue over what Jesus had said, and even his own disciples who had listened attentively, said to each other, 'What an incredible doctrine! Who could possibly accept it?'

Knowing what was in their minds, Jesus said unto them, 'Is it too much for you to accept? What would you think if you saw me, with your own eyes, ascending into heaven? For in time you shall; and to prepare you for such a sight, the Spirit shall beforehand make it all comprehensible to you. At the moment it is beyond your understanding, and even more so it beyond the understanding of all the other people gathered here. The things I have spoken of concern the spirit, which is the essence of even earthly life. The trouble is that even you, some of my followers who should know better, still do not believe me. No one really comes to me unless moved by the Father to do so.'

Slighted by his final remark, many of his followers deserted him, and as Jesus watched them walk away, he turned to the apostles and asked, 'Are you going, too?'

Simon Peter replied, 'To whom would we go? You are the one with knowledge of the everlasting life. We believe, and are convinced that you are truly God's holy son.'

# 24

## *The Sermon on the Mount*

It was about this time, that there took place an incident which was later to become generally known as 'The sermon on the mount'. A great crowd, eager to hear Jesus, had assembled on a gently rising slope and, having seated themselves upon the grass and ceased their idle chatter, Jesus began to speak to them.

'Blessed are those with open minds, for the Kingdom of Heaven shall be theirs. Blessed are they that mourn, for they shall be comforted. Blessed are the meek, for they shall inherit the earth. Blessed are they that hunger and thirst after righteousness, for they shall be satisfied. Blessed are the merciful, for they shall obtain mercy. Blessed are the pure in heart, for they shall see heaven. Blessed are the peacemakers, for they shall be called the children of God. Blessed are they that suffer persecution in defence of righteousness, for they also shall see heaven. Blessed are those who for my sake shall stand up against all such men as shall persecute them and bring all manner of lies and evil slander against them. When this happens, you should rejoice, for you will be in the best of company...the prophets of old were treated in a like manner also, and what a reward shall be waiting for you in heaven.

'You are the salt of the earth, but remember that when salt has lost its flavour it is good for nothing and should be thrown away to be trampled underfoot. You are the light of the world; remember a city that is built on a hill cannot be hid, nor do men light a candle only to hide it under the bed, but instead they set it on a table where it can light the whole room. Likewise let your light shine forth, so that men may see the good works you perform, and glorify the name of God.

'Think not that I have come to destroy the laws of Moses, or the teachings of the prophets, rather have I come to fulfil them. For I assure you that not until the day that heaven and earth pass out of existence, shall the least of the laws be changed, and I warn you that whosoever shall break any of the ten commandments, or shall teach others to do so, then shall he suffer the consequences when passing from his earthly life into that of the spirit world (heaven). Likewise I warn you that to enter the Kingdom of Heaven, your understanding of righteousness and spiritual matters, must at least surpass those of the scribes and Pharisees*.

*(Applies equally to 20th century Christian church leaders.)

'In Mosaic law men are told, "Don't murder". They are also told that a murderer must stand trial, that if a man shows extreme contempt for a brother, he will be accountable to the council of elders, and that the man who calls down a curse upon his brother is liable to the fires of hell. But here is my teaching: I say that if a man is so much as angry at his brother, he is in danger of God's judgement. So, if you happen to be in the synagogue praying, and remember a grievance someone has against you, postpone your praying and go and get things settled peacefully. Then go back to your worship.

'If you are due in court to answer a complaint, settle out of court as soon as you can. If you don't, you may find the plaintiff has brought you before the judge, the judge has sentenced you, and the jailer has put you behind bars. You may be sure that you won't get out until you have paid your debt to the last coin.

'In the law men are told, "Don't commit adultery". But here is my teaching: Adultery isn't simply a physical act...to lust for a woman is to commit adultery with her in your mind.

'In the law men are told that if a man wants to divorce his wife, he must give her a certificate to that effect. But here is my teaching: To divorce a woman on any grounds other than unfaithfulness is to make her an adulteress. Not only that, but any man who marries a divorced woman is an adulterer.

'In the law men are told, "Don't swear falsely in taking an oath, and if you swear an oath to God, carry it out". But here is my teaching: Don't swear an oath of any kind. For instance, don't say "I swear by heaven" because heaven is God's throne. Don't say "I swear by the earth" because the earth is God's footstool. Don't say "I swear by Jerusalem" because Jerusalem is the city of the great king. Nor should you swear "by my head", because you haven't the power to change the colour of a single hair. When you assert something, let your yes be a simple "yes" and your no a simple "no". Anything beyond that has the taint of falsehood.

'In the law men are told, "An eye for an eye and a tooth for a tooth". But here is my teaching: Don't even resist an enemy. If someone hits you on one cheek, then present the other. If someone sues you for your shirt, give it to him...and your robe too. If someone forces you to go a mile with them, go two. If someone demands something of yours, give it to him. If he wants to borrow from you let him, and if he doesn't return it, don't ask for it.

'In the law men are told, "Love thy neighbour and hate your enemies". But here is my teaching: Love your enemies. Be kind to those who hate you, and pray for your persecutors. That's the kind of behaviour that distinguishes God's family. Doesn't God allow the sun to shine equally on good and evil men and doesn't he let the rain fall indiscriminately on both the honest and the dishonest? Treat others the way you would like them to treat you. If you love only those that love you, what is commendable about that?...scoundrels do that. If you are only friendly with your friends, what is exceptional about that?...pagans do that much. If you lend only to those who are a good risk, how is that to your credit?...even the wicked do that. You are to be different. You are to love your enemies, to be good to them, and to lend them money without assurance that you will get it back. Do that and what a reward you will get! Best of all, you will be sons of the Most High. You see, see, in the same way that your heavenly Father is perfect, you also must try to be perfect. In the same way that he is merciful, so you too must be merciful. Your Father is kind even to ingrates and the grasping.

'Take care not to do your good deeds in such a way as to draw attention to yourself...you could lose the reward your Father has for you. When you help people, do it without fanfare, without that ostentation hypocrites employ to gain the admiration of others. The truth is, they've already had all the reward they are going to receive. That way is not for your. When you help someone, don't try to let your left hand know what the right is doing. Keep it secret, and your Father who knows all secrets will reward you.

'Similarly, when you pray, avoid being like the hypocrites who deliberately pray where they will be conspicuous...standing up in a synagogue and out on the street corner. The truth is, public attention is all the reward they will receive. When you pray, go into your room, close the door, and pray privately. Keep it a secret, and your Father who knows all secrets will reward you.

'When you pray don't repeat endless streams of mindless phrases. That is what pagans do. They have the idea that the more they rattle on, the better the prayer. That is not for you. Keep in mind that God is your Father and that he knows what you need, even before you ask. Pray like this:

Our Father who art in heaven,
Hallowed be Thy name,
Thy kingdom come, Thy will be done,
On earth, as it is in heaven.
Grant us each day our daily needs,
And forgive us the wrongs we have done,
As we forgive them who wrong us.
Deliver us from all temptation,
And save us from all evil.
For Thine is the kingdom,
The power and the Glory,
For ever and ever.

Amen

'If you forgive others their wrongs,' Jesus added, 'then your heavenly Father will forgive you yours..if you don't, then he won't.

'Now on the matter of fasting: Don't do as the hypocrites do. What a picture of suffering they present, how woebegone they look...all to draw attention to the fact that they are fasting of course, but you can be sure that that is all the reward they will receive. When you fast, none of that. Keep what you are doing to yourself.

'Don't put away your valuables for your old age: moths may get at them, they could rust or be stolen. Things like that do not happen in heaven, so build up your fortune there. This is where your principal interests truly are.

'The eye is the lens of the body, and if the lens is clear, your body will be flooded with light. But if yours be clouded with greed, the light will not be able to pass through. If where there is light there is darkness, what a darkness it will be.

'No one can be equally loyal to two masters; his loyalties will conflict. Nor can he live for both Almighty God and Mammon. Therefore I say to you, do not waste time worrying about this earthly life, what you should eat, what you should drink, or what you should wear. Is not the life more important than the meat, and the body more importing than clothing? Behold the birds of the air, they do not sow, reap, nor gather food for storage, for they know their heavenly Father feeds them, and are you not more important to Him than they? Which of you by fretting can add even a single second to his life? And if you are not capable of managing that, then what is the point of worrying about other things such as clothes? Learn from the flowers...consider the lilies of the field, how they grow; they do not toil, neither do they spin, yet even Solomon in all his glory was not as magnificently arrayed as they. If God takes such care of even plant-life—things which are here today and gone tomorrow—shall he not care for you even more so? O ye of little faith!

'Therefore take no thought of what to eat, drink, or wear—this is what pagans do. Your heavenly Father has full knowledge of what your needs are. Instead, occupy your thoughts with the Kingdom of God, and His righteousness. Today's problems are problems enough—deal with the problems of tomorrow when tomorrow comes.

'Judge not others, and you also shall not be judged. Overlook their faults, and so too shall your own faults be overlooked. For God will judge you by those same standards which you apply to others. Give freely, and you shall receive twice over.

'Can one blind man lead another blind man?—of course not, they are both likely to end up in a ditch. Does the pupil know more than his master? No, but if he completes his studies he may know as much in time. Why be so concerned about a speck of sawdust in your brother's eye, when you have a whole plank in your own? Do not be a hypocrite—look first to yourself, then perhaps you can look at others.

'Do not give what is holy to dogs (those too ignorant to understand), neither cast pearls (of wisdom) before swine, for they will only trample them underfoot, then turn and attack you.

'Ask and you shall receive, search and you shall find, knock on the door and it shall be opened unto you. I put it to you who are fathers...if your son were to ask your for a piece of bread, would you give him a stone? If he said, "Father, may I have some fish?" would you hand him a snake? Or let us say he asked for an egg, would you hand him a scorpion? Well then, if you, as sinful as you are, shall give your children what they ask for, how much more likely is it that your Father in heaven will give you the Holy Spirit if you ask.

'If everything in the law and teaching of the prophets were reduced to a single sentence, it would be this—treat others as you would have them treat you.

'The gateway to destruction is wide, and the road leading to it is broad and thronged with people. The gateway to life is narrow, as is the road leading to it, and few there are who get through it.

'Be on your guard against the teachers of falsehood. You may easily mistake them for sheep when in fact they are ravenous wolves. How shall you know them?—by the way they live. Grapes do not grow from a thornbush, nor do you find figs on thistles. You pick good fruit from a good tree; you cut down an unproductive tree and burn it. You can judge a good man or a good tree by what each produces.

'Calling me "Lord" shall not give you a place in heaven—only those who actually do the will of my Father in heaven shall gain entry. Many when passing from their earthly body into the spiritual body shall say when coming forward to be judged, "Didn't we preach about you Master? Did we not perform miracles and drive out evil spirits in your name?" Then shall I say to them before the entire assembly, "Go away. You are strangers to me. You have been on the side of evil".

'The difference between those who live by my teaching and those who do not, can be likened to a man who, wishing to build a house, excavates until he strikes rock, then lays the foundation of his house upon that rock. Later, when a violent storm develops and flood waters sweep again t the house, it stands unshaken. This is because it was built on a solid foundation. Those who take no heed to what I say are as foolish as the man who is indifferent to the need for a solid foundation, and built his house on sand. When the storm came, his house was destroyed and swept a way.'

When Jesus had completed his teaching, the people spoke his praises to each other, saying 'Indeed he speaks with an air of authority such as the scribes do not possess.'

As Jesus came down from the mountainside to make his way home, he was suddenly approached by a leper, who fell at his feet saying, 'Lord, if thou willed it so, you could cleanse me of this leprosy.' Putting forth his hand to touch the man, Jesus said, 'I will. Be thou clean,' and immediately the man was cured. Then said Jesus to him, 'Go show thyself to the priest, and offer up the gift that Moses commanded, for a testimony to them.'

Then as Jesus made his way back to Capernaum, a Roman centurion, well known in that city as a good friend to the Jews, having even built them a synagogue, came up to Jesus and said, 'Sir, my servant, to whom I am deeply attached, lies grievously ill with the palsy; please restore him to good health, I beseech you.'

Moved by the centurion's tender concern for his servant, Jesus said, 'I will come with you to your house.'

Then man then said, 'Sir, I am too unworthy to inconvenience you. I know you have only to speak the words, and my servant will be healed. For being a soldier I understand authority; I have superior officers I must obey, just as those who serve beneath me must also carry out my own orders.'

Jesus was very impressed that such a man, and a Roman too, should have such faith in his abilities to cure his servant. 'What faith!' he cried, 'I have not seen faith like this among the Israelites.' Then turning to those around him he said, 'And I tell you now, that many shall come from all the countries of the world to sit with Abraham, Isaac, and Jacob in the Kingdom of Heaven, while those who were the chosen children shall be cast into outer darkness'.

When the centurion returned to his home, he found to his great joy that his beloved servant was fully recovered.

# 25

## *Jesus dines with Simon the Pharisee*

A few days later, in company with his disciples, Jesus set out to visit the city of Nain. As he approached it, he saw a large funeral procession coming through the city gate, and learned that the body was that of a young man, the only son of a poor widow. Seeing how great was the woman's grief, Jesus left the disciples and walking over to her, said, 'Cry no more little mother, for thy son shall he restored to thee.' Then going over to the bier which had been halted, Jesus put his hand upon it and said, 'young man—a rise !' Immediately the young man did so, to the great astonishment of everyone in the procession, and the great joy of his mother.

'A great prophet has come to Israel!' called out one person, whilst another was heard to shout, 'God has come among us.'

As marvellous as were the many acts of healing which Jesus performed around Galilee, many people who had not actually witnessed such things for themselves refused to believe in Jesus, and one day he launched into a bitter denunciation of those towns where he had performed most of his feats of healing, but which had not responded to his teachings.

'How sad for you Chorazin, and for you Bethsaida,' he cried, 'If I had done in Tyre and Sidon what I did in your streets, they would have repented in tears and humility long ago. I warn you, things shall go better for the people of Tyre and Sidon than for you because of your distrust. And you Capernaum, will you be praised?...No, you shall be brought down lower than the level of the ground on which you stand. If Sodom had seen the miracles which you have seen, it would still be standing now. When you people enter the world of spirit and come to be judged, you shall not fare as well as the inhabitants of Sodom.'

Then Jesus paused to pray, saying 'Oh Father, Lord of heaven and earth, praise be to thee that you hide things from the learned and the intelligent, but reveal to them who are childlike.'

Continuing to speak to those around him he said, 'God has entrusted everything to me. No one but the Father really knows who I am, just as I alone know Him...I and those whom I choose to reveal Him to. Therefore come to me all that are weary and heavy with burden, for I can give you rest...listen to my teachings and you shall find complete satisfaction for your every need.'

One day he accepted an invitation to dine at the home of a Pharisee named Simon. Hardly had the meal begun than a woman, well known locally for her notorious immorality, hearing that Jesus was at the house came and knelt at his feet. Tears of repentance flooded from her eyes and fell onto his feet—these she wiped away with her long hair. Then kissing his feet, the woman opened an alabaster flask that she had with her and poured some expensive perfumed onto them, smoothing it in with her hands.

Seeing this happen, Simon said to himself, 'If this man Jesus really is a Prophet, then he would know what a disreputable person this woman is, and he would shun her.' Realising what was passing through Simon's mind, Jesus turned to him and said, 'Simon, I have something I would say to you. There was a certain moneylender who had two debtors, one who owed him five hundred pence, the other fifty. When they could pay him nothing, he graciously forgave both debts. Now tell me Simon, which of these two debtors should be the most grateful?'

Unhesitatingly the Pharisee answered, 'Why of course the man who had been forgiven the most!'

'Exactly so,' said Jesus. Then turning to the woman at his feet, he said, 'Look at this woman. When I entered your house Simon, you gave me no water with which to wash the dust from my feet, yet this woman has wet them with her tears, and dried them with her hair. Nor did you give me a kiss of welcome, but this woman has not ceased kissing my feet since she entered the room. You offered me no oil to anoint my head, yet this woman has perfumed my feet. Therefore Simon I tell you this: her sins, as many as they might be, are forgiven because her love is so great. According to the measure of each person's love, so shall forgiveness be meted out to them.'

Then turning to the woman, Jesus said, 'Your faith has saved you. Go in peace, and sin no more.'

Many of Simon's guests (also Pharisees), on hearing Jesus forgive the woman, immediately turned to each other saying, 'Who is this man that he dares to think that he can forgive sins.'

# 26

### *The Master instructs his disciples*

It was about this time that Jesus again decided he should send out some of the disciples on their own, and calling them together he blessed them and gave them their instructions.

'You are to go out empty-handed' he said, 'take neither money nor food. You are to go as you stand, with no more than the clothes you are wearing and the sandals you have on your feet: a good workman need never fear that he will not be recompensed.

'When first you arrive in a strange town, discover the name of some worthy person with whom you can stay until you are ready to depart. When first you enter their house, bless it: if it is a good house, then your blessing will be returned to you. If anyone refuses to offer you hospitality, or a town rejects your message, then leave: and as you go, stamp your feet to shake off the dust of the place, and make it clear to the people of that place how badly you have been treated. You may be sure of one thing, they will not fare as well as the people of Sodom and Gomorrah when they pass in to spirit.

'You are going out in to the world with no more defences that a sheep would have amid a pack of wolves, so be as wary as a snake and as guileless as a dove. Always be on your guard, for always there will be men who seek to have you arrested and delivered up to the councils, and will haul you into their synagogues to be flogged. Because of your loyalty to me, you will be dragged before governors and kings...though this shall give you, in fact, an opportunity to explain to them your faith.

'When your enemies have delivered you up, worry not as to how you should defend yourself or what you should say, for when the time comes, God's spirit shall put the appropriate words into your mouth.

'A time shall come when, because of me, brother shall betray brother, fathers shall betray their children, and children shall turn against their parents, even though doing so shall cost them their own life. As disciples of me you will be hated by many, but stay true to me and you shall be delivered. If you are persecuted in a certain city, then leave it and go on to another. Believe me, before you have had time to go through all the cities of Israel, the son of man will have returned.

' The disciple is not above his master, nor the servant above his lord,' continued Jesus. 'It is enough that they become like them. For if they call me Beelzebub, what pray shall they call you? But fear them not, for every secret shall be revealed, and what I now tell in the dark you shall repeat in daylight, and things which I am obliged at this time to tell you in whispers, you shall in time shout from the roof-tops.

'Never fear those who may have the power to kill your earthly body but no power to kill your soul. Instead fear the one who has the power to destroy both your body and soul in hell.

'Cannot two sparrows be bought for a penny? Yet not a single sparrow falls to the ground without your Father's knowledge . This being so, bear in mind that you have greater value to the Father than a whole flock of sparrows. If you boldly declare yourself a follower of me in public, then when the time comes and you pass into spirit, I also shall stand up for you in the presence of the Father; repudiate me here, and I shall do the same to you in heaven.

'Think not that my coming will bring peace on earth; on the contrary, my coming creates dissension, as you have already seen. There will be dissension between son and father, between daughter and mother, and between in-laws. If your loyalty to your parents comes before your loyalty to me, then you do not deserve to be a member of my family. The same is true if you prefer a son or daughter before me. Nor are you worthy of me if you are not prepared to die for me. He that hangs on too tightly to his earthly life on my account shall find a life of eternal brightness in the spirit world.

‘ All who welcome you are welcoming me, and they that welcome me, welcome the God who sent me. It is like this: he that welcomes a prophet because he is a prophet, shall receive a prophet’s reward, and he that welcomes a righteous man because he is a righteous man, shall receive a righteous man’s reward. Likewise whosoever shall give you simply a drink of water because you are followers of me, then you can be sure that he too shall also be rewarded.’

Having thus instructed the disciples, Jesus sent them out in pairs to preach and to teach the news of God’s kingdom. They also healed the sick (which is the duty of every true follower of Christ) and sought to drive out evil spirits.

The fact that more and more people were flocking to hear Jesus and his followers caused increasing concern to certain officials in Jerusalem, and they sought to find fault with him and his teachings at every opportunity. There was for example an occasion when a delegation of Pharisees and Sadducees had come from Jerusalem to see Jesus, and noticed that his followers ate without first washing their hands; it had long been a Jewish custom to wash the hands carefully before eating, and to clean cups, pots and pans with great care.

Seizing the opportunity to make criticism, one of the Pharisees remarked, ‘Why do your followers flout the teaching of the elders by not washing their hands before meals?’

‘Why do you flout the commandments of God?’ countered Jesus. ‘Moses instructed you to honour your father and your mother, but you teach that it is permissible for a man to say to needy parents, “I cannot help you, for what I might have given to you has been dedicated to God”. Thus your doctrines replace the will of God. You hypocrites,’ cried Jesus, ‘Isaiah surely had such as you in mind, when he wrote:

> These people talk of great faith,
> But they practise not what they preach.
> Their worship is a fruitless thing,
> Their teaching is the precepts of men.

'It is not that which goes into a man's mouth that defiles him, but that which come out of it.'

Angered by the remarks of Jesus, the delegation of Pharisees and Sadducees immediately returned to Jerusalem. As they withdrew, one of Jesus's followers said to him, 'Master you have offended the Pharisees with what you have said.' Jesus answered, 'Every plant my heavenly Father has not planted, shall be uprooted. These Pharisees are blind, and the leaders of the blind.'

Then said Peter, 'What meant you that a man was defiled only by what came out of his mouth, and not by what went into it?'

Jesus, a little surprised that even Peter was not able to understand his meaning, said, 'Do you still not realize that what goes into a man's mouth simply passes to his belly, and then is cast out by the bowels.' (So saying he automatically removed all foods from the ' unclean' list). 'But the things that come out of a man's mouth spring forth from his heart, and it is these which defile him. For from his heart come evil thoughts of murder, adulteries, fornications, thefts, lies and blasphemies. These are the things which defile a man...not eating with unwashed hands!'

Leaving Galilee, Jesus and his followers now made their way to Tyre and Sidon. News of his presence in those cities quickly spread, and he was visited by a certain woman from Canaan, who cried out, 'O Lord, son of David, my daughter is possessed of an evil spirit; please come and exorcise her.'

To test the strength of the woman's faith, Jesus ignored her request, but the woman would not be put off, and began pestering the disciples, trying to enlist their help in the matter. Eventually the disciples also appealed to Jesus on her behalf, but he said, 'My Father sent me only to seek the lost sheep of Israel.' Then the woman herself again came to plead with him, but Jesus only said, 'Should I give to the dogs what is intended for the children of Israel?' being aware that in fact Jesus had already healed many who were Gentiles, the woman replied, 'Lord, even dogs are allowed to eat the crumbs that fall from their master's table.' Moved by her persistence and determination, Jesus said, 'Woman, great is they faith, thy wish is granted.' When the woman returned home, she found to her great joy that the evil spirit had already departed from her daughter.

# 27

*The spirit revealed in all its glory*

One day when Jesus had been touring through some villages in Caesarea Philippi with the apostles, he paused to say a few prayers, and afterwards he put a question to them. 'Who do the people think I am?' he asked.

' Some say you are John the Baptist, others that you are Elijah. Others think you must be one of the other great prophets returned from the grave,' they said.

'And who do you think I am?' Jesus asked.

Without hesitation, Peter quickly answered, ' Master you are the Christ, the son of the Living God!'

Well pleased with Peter's reply, Jesus said, 'blessed are you Simon Peter, for no human could have revealed such to you...only my Father who is in heaven. Therefore Peter, you are the foundation on which my church shall be built, and I will give you the key to all knowledge relating to both this material world and the world of spirit, God's heavenly kingdom. All judgements you make, shall he made under guidance of the heavenly Father.' Then Jesus gave Peter and the others strict instructions to keep secret the fact that he was the Christ.

It was from that time on, that Jesus began hinting to his followers that the time was drawing near, when the would have to go to Jerusalem, there to endure great suffering, stand trial by the elders, the chief priests and scribes, and eventually suffer execution at their hands. On one occasion when he referred to these future events publicly, Peter took him aside saying, 'Never, Master. This must never happen to you.'

To Peter's surprise, Jesus at once rebuked him, saying, 'Get thee behind me Satan. Now you disappoint me by behaving like a man, and not as an instrument of God.'

Then turning towards his followers again, he said, 'If you wish to truly follow me, you must be prepared not only to deny yourself your own desires, but to die for your faith if need be. He who holds life too precious will most certainly lose it, while the man who is prepared to give his earthly life for my sake shall find eternal life in the next phase of existence (the spirit world). What is so wonderful about this short earthly existence, that you would trade your eternal life for it?

'If you are ashamed to be identified with me and my teachings at a time as wicked and unfaithful as the present, then sh all I deny knowledge of you when you pass from this life and enter the world of spirit, for then shall you be judged by what you have done here and now.'

Six days later, Jesus took the three apostles nearest and dearest to him, Peter, James and John high up Mount Hermon, and there amid the peace and tranquillity of nature, Jesus was to prepare their minds for his forthcoming 'death' and resurrection. Knowing that words were not sufficient to convey a real understanding to them, Jesus had decided on a practical demonstration for these chosen few.

The rarified mountain air, combined with the stillness and increasing darkness , made the perfect setting for a seance, and soon all were sinking deeper and deeper into a trance. After a considerable while, Peter, James and John slowly began to come out of their deep sleep-like state, and as they did so they were aware that the whole appearance of Jesus had now changed, his face and robes having become radiantly bright and glistening, as if lit from within. As they stared in awe and wonder, they also became aware that two other figures were standing with Jesus, equally dazzling in appearance, and from the conversation taking place between these bright and glorified beings, it became clear that Jesus was in fact speaking with none other than Moses and Elijah.

Jesus, having dematerialised his body and shown himself in all the glory of his spiritual body, thereby acquainted these chosen apostles with its appearance, thus making him more recognisable when the time should come for him to show himself to them after his crucifixion; and indeed as the apostles listened to the conversation of the three holy beings, the topic was the impending visit of Jesus to Jerusalem, and his departure from the earth.

The impact on the apostles was staggering, and the presence of Moses the lawgiver and Elijah the prophet corroborated all that Jesus had previously told them. So excited was Peter by what was happening, that he wished all the other apostles to share in the experience as well, and so in an effort to detain Moses and Elijah longer he suggested he construct small shelters for them, from the branches of nearby trees, to protect them from the cold.

However, even as he was speaking, the three brilliant figures slowly began to dematerialise, disappearing into a cloud of bright ectoplasm. As this took place, a voice was heard to say. 'This is my beloved son, in whom I am well pleased. Listen to him.'

Completely overwhelmed by it all, the apostles now fell to the ground trembling with fear, but a moment later they heard the voice of Jesus saying, 'Get up. There is no need to fear.' Looking up, they saw that Jesus had resumed his earthly appearance, and the cloud of bright ectoplasm had completely disappeared.

As they all walked down the mountainside together, Jesus said to the apostles, 'See that you do not speak to the others about that which you saw here on the mountain this night. Not until I am resurrected, shall you speak of this to anyone.'

Then the disciples asked, 'What do the scribes mean when they say that Elijah must reappear before the Messiah shall come?'

Jesus answered, 'Because it is true. Elijah must come first to make a path for the Messiah...to prepare the way. But perhaps you are wondering how the prophets could possibly write that the Messiah would be subjected to suffering and scorn? In fact Elijah has already come, and as was truly predicted they did their worst to him, and I too shall suffer at their hands.' Having thought about Jesus's reply, the disciples realised that he had in fact been referring to John the Baptist.

When they had all reached the foot of the mountain the following morning, they found their fellow disciples surrounded by a large crowd and arguing with some scribes. Those that saw Jesus was approaching, ran excitedly to welcome him.

'What is the matter?' he asked.

One man fell at the feet of Jesus and said, 'Sir, my son suffers from epileptic fits, he is also deaf and dumb, and hearing that you were in the district, I brought my son to be cured by you. However on arrival, I found you were not here, so instead sought the aid of your disciples, only to discover that they could do nothing to help my son. Please Master, say you will help him.'

Turning to the disciples Jesus cried, 'O ye of little faith! How long shall I remain with you, and put up with you?' Then to the man at his feet he said. ' Rise and bring your son to me.'

As the boy was brought forward, he suddenly fell to the ground in a convulsion, threshing about and foaming at the mouth. 'How long has he been like this?' asked Jesus.

'Ever since he was little more than a babe,' replied the Father, 'We shall be forever grateful if you can help him.'

Jesus answered, 'It is not what I can do...can you believe? Everything is possible for the man who has faith and believes.'

'I do, I do,' cried the man.

Jesus, then bending low over the boy, touched him, saying, 'Evil spirit, depart and leave this boy in peace.' Immediately the lad rose to his feet, completely cured, and after offering up a prayer of thanks to God, the man took his son by the hand and led him home.

'Why were we unable to cure the lad?' asked one of the disciples.

'Because you lacked sufficient faith,' Jesus replied. 'If you had faith no larger than a mustard seed, then would you be able to say to a mountain. "Move from here to there", and this would be done. Nothing is impossible for those with faith.'

A few days later, while they were all staying in Capernaum, the temple tax-collector came to receive the tribute money, asking of Peter, 'Does your Master pay tribute money?'

'Of course he does,' replied Peter, and straight away went into the house to fetch the money. However, before he could pay the tax-collector, Jesus stopped him, saying, 'Peter when kings wish to extract money, from whom do they take it?—their own family, or others?'

'From Others,' answered Peter.

'Then the "family" of God should not have to pay temple taxes, ' said Jesus. 'But let us not offend them and give them more cause to complain against us; go down to the lake Peter, throw in a fishing-line and in the mouth of the first fish you catch, you shall find a coin with which to pay the tax.' Following his Master's instruction, Peter caught a fish and, sure enough, just as Jesus had said, there in its mouth was a coin to pay the tax-man.

Another day the twelve apostles were arguing amongst themselves, who would hold the more important posts in heaven when they passed to spirit, and Jesus came to see what the dispute was about. All were reluctant to speak but Jesus, knowing what was in their minds, said, 'Those who seek position through selfishness shall find themselves serfs in the Kingdom of Heaven; only the truly meek and humble shall wear crowns of glory.' Then seeing a small child nearby he called the child to him, and sitting it on his lap he said to his followers, 'Not until you change your ways of thinking, and have the same humility and simple trust of this little one, can you ever hope to aspire to anything in heaven. Who shall be the greatest? None other but the humblest!'

'Master,' said John, 'while we were on the road here earlier today, we encountered a man driving evil spirits from people, and using your name as his authority for doing so. Since he was not one of our group, we told him to stop at once.'

'You should not have done that,' said Jesus. 'All who do good works in my name are to be encouraged. It is those who use my name to lead people along the paths of sinfulness who should beware; it would be better for all such men as this to tie a millstone round their necks and then throw themselves into the deepest part of the lake.

'If thy foot or thy hand offend thee, then cut them off and cast them away. It is better to go through your earthly life in a maimed condition than spend your eternal spirit-life in the realms of never ending darkness. Likewise if thy eye offend thee, then pluck it out and cast it away, for it is better to leave this earthly life half blind, than spend your eternal life in the realms of the damned.'

Then looking down at the little child on his lap, Jesus said, 'See that you never disdain one of these little ones. They have angels who are never far from God's presence.'

'Now I wish to put a question to you,' said Jesus, looking at the apostles gathered round him.' If a man owns one hundred sheep, and one of them wanders off and is lost, would he not leave the ninety-nine and go looking for the lost one? And, having found it, would he not be happier for that one than all the ninety-nine that had not strayed? So is it with these little ones; your Father has no wish to lose one of them either.

'If your brother has done you harm, go to him and discuss the matter with him. If he listens, and makes amends, your relationship can be mended. But if he refuses to listen, you should not despair that in time your brother may mend his ways and relent.'

Peter then asked, ' Master, with regard to a brother who does me wrong; how many times should I forgive him—seven times?'

Jesus answered, 'Not seven times, but seventy-seven times. Let me give you a little example of how things work in the kingdom. Here is a king settling up accounts with his indentured servants, and one of these, to whom he has loaned a thousand gold coins, is unable to repay the loan. The man begs for more time to pay and the king, full of understanding, not only forgives the debt but also allows the man his freedom. Yet this same servant, once freed from his obligations, goes straight to a fellow servant owing him just ten gold coins and threatens him with prison unless he makes good his debt. The man pleads with him but, unmoved, the wicked servant has his poor fellow-worker thrown into prison. Hearing of the servant's uncharitable behaviour, the king immediately has him arrested and brought before him, saying, 'You miserable wretch! I forgave your debt because you pleaded with me, yet you show no such sympathy for your fellow servant who owes you money.' Then angrily the king ordered that the man be jailed until such time as his debt was fully repaid.

'Thus,' said Jesus, 'shall my father treat all of you who refuse to forgive your brother, and forgive him from the heart.'

## 28

### *Jesus sets out for Jerusalem*

Now the feast of the Tabernacles was approaching, and some of Jesus's followers, who were politically minded and had no real understanding of what Jesus taught, suggested this was an ideal time to go into Judaea saying, 'Surely anyone wishing to increase his fame and become a well known public figure should not keep his message secret. Why not let the people of Judaea become acquainted with the marvellous things you are capable of?'

But Jesus, knowing full well their motives were personal and materialistic, was reluctant to enter Judaea at that time, saying, 'No, the time is not yet ripe for me, though it is always the right time for people such as yourselves. The world has no reason to hate you, but I prick the conscience of so many who set themselves up as pious leaders of the people, that they despise me, and would seek to destroy me...I shall go to Jerusalem, but not just yet.' Hearing this, a large number of his followers went on to the city ahead of him.

When Jesus finally decided the time had come for him to start the journey, he did not join one of the many caravans going in that direction but went privately, with just a few of his chosen disciples. Arriving in one Samaritan village they immediately set about seeking shelter for the night. However the villagers, knowing full well the identity of Jesus and fearing the wrath of the religious leaders in Jerusalem should they learn that he had been offered hospitality, refused to accommodate him and his followers.

In a furious temper, James and John cried out, 'Master, shall we call down fire from heaven to incinerate them?' But having strongly rebuked them for the attitude which they had taken on the matter, Jesus said they should continue their journey to the next village.

News quickly spread to Jerusalem that Jesus was on his way, and throughout the city he became a general topic of conversation and the subject of much argument; for while there were many to praise the wondrous things he had done, there were others who feared that what he taught was in contradiction to their religious leaders in the temple, and might in any case interfere too much with their own selfish style of living.

By the time Jesus arrived in Jerusalem, the festival was at its height, and he went directly to the temple where he immediately began teaching, huge crowds quickly gathering round to listen to this controversial figure.

'Let me first tell you how I have such knowledge of all the things I discuss,' began Jesus. 'It is because I speak not my own thoughts, but the wisdom of Him who sent me. If you too are prepared to do his bidding, then you will at once know that the thoughts I project come not from me, but from God. A teacher who simply presents his own poor thoughts and opinions seeks only vain glory for himself, but the man who seeks only to honour God speaks the truth without deceit. Moses gave you laws, but do any of you fully observe them? Why then are there those among you who would seek to kill me because I do so?'

'You are mad,' called someone in the crowd. 'No one seeks to harm you!'

'If that be so,' said Jesus,'why it is that some of you become so angered when I heal a man on the sabbath Day? Moses established circumcision as law amongst you, and for your own convenience you circumcise a boy on the sabbath. Seek not to judge things only by their outward appearances, but by their inner substance.'

After Jesus had completed his teaching for that day, and departed for his lodgings, there was much speculation among those who had listened to him. 'If the temple authorities are seeking to destroy this man Jesus,' one said, 'is it not strange that they allow him to speak openly, right in the temple itself? Can he really be the Christ?'

'How can you dare to suggest such a thing? others retorted. The Messiah, when he comes, will be a great and powerful prince...not a son of a carpenter from Nazareth!'

'Knowing what was said of him amongst the people of Jerusalem, Jesus raised the subject one day as he taught in the temple. 'Many of you think you know where I come from,' he said. 'I am not here of my own choosing, but come as a representative of the one true God, and I am His messenger.'

Some people reasoned with each other, 'This man has performed many miraculous feats and cures, what ordinary man could do such things? Could even this Messiah, when he comes, do greater things?'

This growing speculation throughout the city, and the increasing popularity of Jesus right under the noses of the chief priests, at last began to seriously alarm them and they sent out a detachment of temple guards to arrest him.

The people were puzzled when Jesus said to them, 'I shall be with you only a short while, then I must return to Him who sent me. You may look for me, but where I am going, you will be unable to follow.'

'What can he mean?' the people asked each other. ' Does he mean that he is intending to depart for Greece or Alexandria? Is he going there to teach?'

It was the last day of the festival, and standing up in the temple Jesus cried out, 'If there are any who are thirsty for the truth, then let them come to me. Put your faith in me and, just as the Scriptures say, you shall have a source of living water within you.'

Aroused and inspired by his oratory and his teaching, the crowds grew restless and unruly, and they began to argue with each other, some saying, 'Indeed this man is a great prophet, maybe even the Christ we were told to expect, while others sneeringly said, 'A Christ from Galilee? How preposterous! The prophets told that the Messiah would come from Bethlehem, "The city of king David", and would be a descendant of David.'

So heated became the various opinions of the people that even the guards sent to arrest Jesus joined in, and found themselves siding with his supporters to such an extent that they refused to carry out the arrest.

When the guards returned to the chief priest in the council chamber without Jesus, the Pharisees were furious, cursing the guards and shouting, 'Have you been duped as well? How could you have been such fools as to agree with the rabble; do you think we, your religious leaders, are the better judges of this man, this false prophet?'

It was then that one of the council members, a man named Nicodemus, stood up and said, 'Are we condemning this man without first hearing his defence, or even the charges?' What kind of justice is this?' Nicodemus had himself spoken with 'Jesus on one occasion, and had been deeply impressed by his quiet and humble dignity and his inspiring message of love and peace.

The other members of the council, stunned and very angry that one of their own number should stand up in defence of Jesus, shouted, 'Are you too from Galilee? Where in the Scriptures does it say the Christ shall come from Galilee?' And without waiting for Nicodemus to reply, they all filed out of the chamber.

Jesus, having spent the night praying and meditating on the Mount of Olives, early next morning returned once more to the temple, and being immediately surrounded by a large crowd, he began to teach. The scheming scribes and Pharisees, seeking ways to trap Jesus and bring charges against him, said, 'Now teacher, what judgement would you make on this woman? She is an adulteress, caught in the very act of her sin. The law of Moses states that she should be stoned to death, but what do you say?'

Knowing full well their efforts to trick him, Jesus replied, 'If you consider it a just punishment, then stone her. 'But', he added, 'let him who has never sinned throw the first stone!'

Jesus had made his point, and those who had only a few moments before been feeling so self-righteous, now slowly and self-consciously began to slink away, one by one. Waiting a few minutes, he then turned to the woman and said, 'Where are your accusers? Is there no one left to condemn you?'

'Not one, Master,' the woman replied.

'Then nor shall I,' said Jesus, 'Now go and sin no more.'

A little later that day, teaching a crowd near the Treasury, Jesus said, 'I am the light of the world, and he that follows me shall never walk in darkness.' Thinking this a most arrogant statement to make, a Pharisee sarcastically cried out, 'Self-recommendation is hardly to be a trusted!'

'That does not alter the fact that I speak the truth,' said Jesus. 'I know my source, and I know my destination. You do not. You are ready to criticize me; I criticize no one, but if I did, my judgement would be fair because it would be inspired by Almighty God who sent me.'

A little later in his teaching Jesus repeated something he had already spoken of earlier, 'Soon I shall be leaving you, and where I go you cannot follow—at least not yet.'

'What does he mean?' they asked each other, 'Where is he going?' Realizing that they were not capable of understanding his meaning, he explained further 'You and I may look alike, but we are not. You are of this world, I am not.'

'Who are you then?' they asked, even more puzzled than ever.

Jesus answered, 'I am who I have said I am all along—the son of God the Father. When you lift me up (upon the Cross), then will you know that I have not acted of my own accord, but upon the instructions of Him who is my Father. He is ever with me, and my only desire is to serve him.'

By now many people in the crowd were ready to believe in him, and to them he said, 'Follow my teachings, and the truth shall not only be made clear to you, but also set you free.'

A Pharisee hearing this at once objected, saying, 'What mean you. We shall be set free. We are descendants of Abraham and have never been slaves to any man!'

'Once again you display your shallow thinking,' replied Jesus. 'I am not suggesting that you are the slaves of men, but the slaves of sin. You may be the descendants of Abraham, but you dishonour him by rejecting me.'

'How can we possibly be dishonouring Abraham by rejecting you? ' said the man.

'Because Abraham was a faithful servant of God, and since God my Father has sent met to you, Abraham would expect you to receive me with full honour, respect and love. Do you know,' continued Jesus, 'Why you are not capable of understanding my teachings? It is because you are not capable of understanding the truth; lies and deceit are the only things you understand. I make you a challenge! Can any of you here present charge me with any sin No? Then why when I tell you the truth do you disbelieve me?'

'Is not the real truth that you are a Samaritan possessed by a devil?' called out someone.

'Does one devil exorcize other devils as I have done?' asked Jesus. 'No, my purpose here is to honour my Father, you are here this day to try and dishonour me. The fact remains, he that follows my teachings will never die.'

'Now we know you are mad! ' shouted a man in the crowd. 'Abraham is dead, and so are all the prophets, yet you say that anyone who follows your teachings will live for ever; are you greater even than Abraham and all the prophets? They all died; how are you any different to they?'

'Your Father, Abraham rejoiced in anticipation of my coming, hundreds of years ago, and now that he has seen this happen he is glad,' said Jesus.

Staggered by this last remark, someone said, 'But you are less than forty years old. How could you possibly have seen Abraham?'

'The truth is,' Jesus replied, ' that I existed before Abraham was born.'

So enraged were many of the people now, by what they considered this man's audacity, that the began picking up stones and hurling them at him, and would have attempted to kill him had not the disciples helped him to escape unharmed.

A few days later Jesus was out walking with his followers, when they came upon a beggar who had been blind from birth. 'Master,' said one of the followers, 'Why was this man born blind?'

'So that he might be yet one more example of God's power,' said Jesus, and going over to the man, Jesus bent down, spat in the dust, and making a little mud, spread the dust, and making a little mud, spread the mixture onto the beggar's eyes. 'Now go and wash it off in the nearby pool, and your sight shall be given to you,' said Jesus.

Doing as he had been instructed, to his great joy the beggar found that he could now see for the first time in his life. Almost at once people began remarking, 'Isn't that the beggar who used to be blind? But how is it that he is blind no longer?'

Hearing them, the beggar replied, 'The man they call Jesus was responsible, He put mud on my eyes then told me to wash it off; I did, any my sight was given to me in that instant.'

Since this had happened on a sabbath, a group of the people led the beggar to some Pharisees and repeated to them what had happened. ' This man Jesus is an evil man if he breaks the sabbath law,' said one, though another said. 'How is it possible he can do such miracles of goodness if he is evil?' Turning to the beggar himself, the Pharisees said, 'Tell us, what do you think of this man Jesus? '

'I think he is a great prophet,' the beggar replied.

Determined to think only ill of Jesus, the Pharisees refused to believe that the beggar had in fact been blind from birth in the first place, so they sent for the man's parents for confirmation. Learning that the beggar had indeed spoken the truth, they then asked his parents if they were aware of who had healed their son. The old couple, knowing that the authorities had agreed to ban anyone from the synagogue who gave credit to Jesus for any of the feats of healing he had done, hesitated, then said, 'We do not know. Ask our son, he is old enough to speak for himself!'

Turning to the beggar once more, the Pharisees said, 'Surely you must give credit to God for the return of your sight, not this evil man Jesus?'

'The only thing I know,' said the beggar, 'is that I used to be blind, and now I can see.'

Still intent on making some charge against Jesus, the Pharisees then said, 'Very well, but explain to us exactly what this Jesus did and said.'

Exasperated, the poor beggar answered, 'I have told you already; how many more time times must I tell you?'

'You are trying to protect this Jesus!' cried the Pharisees, 'We follow the teaching of Moses, and everyone knows where he got his instructions from...from God.'

With surprising cleverness of thought (clearly inspired by God), the beggar spoke up in defence of this man to whom he was so extremely grateful, saying, 'We are all aware that God does works of goodness only through good people. Do you know of any other man, blind from birth, who has regained his sight? If Jesus were not sent from God, he could not have done this thing.'

Boiling with rage that yet one more attempt to bring charges against Jesus had failed, the priests and Pharisees hurled insults at the beggar, and had him thrown out of the synagogue.

Hearing what had happened, Jesus went looking for the beggar, and having found him said, 'Do you believe in the son of God?'

'Tell me who he is, Master,' said the beggar.

'Not only have you seen him, he is talking to you,' Jesus replied. Immediately the beggar knelt at the feet of Jesus, and worshipped him. As he did so, Jesus said, 'I have come that those with two good eyes might have them opened.'

A Pharisee overhearing this remark, said, 'Are you suggesting that we are blind?'

'Your guilt lies in the fact that you insist you can see.'

Then Jesus began to tell a parable to those around him. 'Here is a sheep pen, with a gate. So that if you see a man sneaking into the pen some other way, then you can be sure he is a thief. When the shepherd wishes to enter, he goes to the proper entrance. The sheep know the sound of the true shepherd's voice and will follow his. A false shepherd has difficulty in keeping the sheep together, and will even desert his flocks when a wolf comes and scatters them. A true shepherd is ready to lay down his life for his sheep...just as I shall do.'

'Teacher,' said a man, 'How can I ensure eternal life?'

Jesus answered, 'What says the law on the subject?'

'The law demands that I love God with all that I am,' the man replied, 'my will, my spirit, my body, and my intellect. It also demands that I have the same regard for my neighbour as for myself.'

'Then you already know the answer!' said Jesus.

The man then said, 'But who is my neighbour?'

Once again, as was his general custom, Jesus gave his reply in the form of a parable. 'A certain man is making a journey from Jerusalem to Jericho. On the way he is attacked by thieves, who steal his money, take his clothes, then beat him until he is half-dead, then leave him lying by the road-side. Shortly afterwards a priest comes along and seeing the man passes by on the other side of the road. The comes a Levite, and he also passes the man by. Next comes one of the despised Samaritans. Seeing the man lying there, he feels sorry for him, and going to him bathes his wounds with oil and wine, then bandages him. Then, putting the man on his own mule, he takes him to a roadside inn where he lodges the man and cares for him. Next morning, after settling his account with the inn-keeper, he says to him 'Please do all you can for this poor man while I am gone. Give him whatever he needs and I will take care of his bill on my return journey.'

'Now,' said Jesus, 'of the three men travelling along that road—the priest, the Levite, and the Samaritan,—which one showed a neighbourly spirit?'

'The one who gave aid,' said the man.

'Then go, and do you likewise,' replied Jesus.

Arriving in the village of Bethany with a few of his followers, Jesus made his way to the house of a woman named Martha. Having welcomed him and his disciples into her home, Martha then went into the kitchen to prepare a meal for all of them. While she did so, her sister Mary sat at the feet of Jesus, listening while he talked to those around him. With so much food to prepare and cook, Martha grew increasingly annoyed when her sister made no attempt to come and help here. Finally she went into the room where Jesus sat, and said, 'Master, please tell Mary that it is her duty to come and help me in the kitchen.'

'Calm yourself Martha,' said Jesus, 'you must not allow such things to upset you. Only one thing really matters, and Mary has got her priorities right, I am pleased to say.'

## 29

### *The raising of Lazarus*

On one of his many tours through the towns and villages of Galilee one day, a man called out to him, 'Teacher, my brother has come into a legacy, but refused to share it with me. Please order him to do so.'

Jesus replied, 'I have no authority to give such an order, and in any case, who made me your judge?'

Turning to other people who had gathered around, Jesus then said, 'Guard against greed. There is more to life than simply accumulating earthly wealth. Let me tell you a story. There was once a wealthy farmer whose yield of grain had been so great for three consecutive years, that he simply did not have enough barns to store it all in. "What on earth am I going to do with it all?" he thought, "I shall just have to build another big new barn. I shall be so rich, and my whole future will now be secure," but then the voice of God spoke to him and said, "You foolish man, tonight you are to die...now who will benefit from all this wealth?"

' That is how it is with men who are rich in material things, but impoverished in spiritual things,' said Jesus, and turning to his disciples he added, 'This is why I am continually emphasising how unimportant are the transient things of life. Likewise do not put off until tomorrow those works of charity and deeds of goodness which you should be attending to today; who knows if you will ever see tomorrow? And those lucky people to whom God has entrusted a knowledge of the spirit, owe it to him to pass on this understanding to all their less fortunate brothers and sisters. Much is expected from a man who has been so honoured with a knowledge of the spirit, for it has been im parted to him not solely for his own benefit, but for the benefit and development of all mankind. Those who receive the knowledge but neglect to pass it on have much to answer for when they pass over. I myself have come to light a fire here on earth,' said Jesus, 'How I wish it were already ablaze.'

As he finished speaking, some men hurried up and told him that some soldiers of the Roman governor, Pilate, had just butchered some Galileans while they were at worship in the temple. 'Are you thinking that these were the worst men in Galilee, and that was why they suffered such a fate?' asked Jesus. 'Unless you all mend your ways, you will all meet a fate just as terrible when you pass into the spirit world.'

Then Jesus related another of his parables. 'There was once a man who had a fig tree in his garden, and from time to time he would check to see if any figs had been produced. One day he called his gardener to him and said, "For three years I have looked to this fig tree for fruit, but in all that time it has given nothing, therefore chop it down, for it is taking up valuable space that could be put to better use." The gardener replied, "Give it one more year. I will cultivate and fertilize it, and we will see what happens. If it is still barren after that, well then it can be chopped down".'

A moment later a group of Pharisees came along, and cried out to Jesus, 'You had best leave this district while you still can...Herod is out to kill you.'

'Go tell that Fox that I intend to remain here until my work is finished,' said Jesus, ' though I shall not be arrested here. It would not suit my purpose to die outside of Jerusalem.'

Moving to another area a few days later, Jesus received an invitation to dine with a prominent Pharisee in the district, on a sabbath day. A number of other Pharisees and some lawyers were present, including one man suffering from dropsy.

During the meal, Jesus posed a question: 'Is it permissible in law to heal on the sabbath?' No one answered, and so Jesus put his hands on the man with dropsy, and healed him.

Then Jesus said 'I have another question I would put to you. Which of you if your mule or ox fell into a ditch on a sabbath, would not pull it out?' Again no one responded.

Earlier, when the guests had been assembling for the meal, Jesus had noticed how the guests jostled each other for the more prominent seats, and he began to relate a parable to them. 'When invited to a wedding feast, let me advise you not to take the best seat. Some more distinguish your seat and move further down. How much better to take a poorer seat on arrival, and then later when your host invites you to take a better seat you will be honoured in front of everyone. Exalt yourself, and you shall be put down—even as the humble shall be honoured.'

Then turning to his host Jesus said, 'Giving such a dinner as this, and inviting all your friends, family and wealthy neighbours, is no act of goodness or kindness, since most likely all those present will at some time or other invite you to dine with them in return. Instead you should invite the crippled, the lame, and the blind to your table; not only will you derive much satisfaction from this gesture, but you will be rewarded for your kindness when you enter the Kingdom of Heaven'.

One day when Jesus was speaking to a large number of people who had gathered around him, he spoke regarding the problems confronting would-be disciples. 'It is not easy to become a disciple of mine,' he warned, 'four you allegiance to me must come before everything else in your life...parents, brothers, sisters, wives and children. Indeed you must be prepared to give the very breath of life itself, if need be, to defend my name.

'If you were going to build a house, you would hardly begin work on its erection until you had first made sure that you had sufficient funds to complete it, would you? The same applies to those contemplating life as one of my disciples.'

Among the crowds that came to hear Jesus speak every day, there were always a great many of the outcast and disreputable amongst them. Noticing this, the Pharisees said 'Why does this Jesus mix and associate with so many people?...Why, he even takes meals with them!'

Hearing the comments that had been made, Jesus told the following parable: ' There was once a certain woman whose whole wealth amounted to no more than ten silver coins. One day she lost one of them, and although perhaps a trifling amount to some people, the one silver coin represented a great deal to the woman concerned, and she made a very thorough search for it. In the end her patience was rewarded, and so delighted was she that she called in all her friends and neighbours, said "Come celebrate with me, for I have found the coin which I lost." Then Jesus said, 'I tell you now, that the whole of heaven rejoices when even a single sinner is turned away from corruption and saved.'

Then Jesus told another story: 'There was a man with two sons, the younger of whom came to him one day saying, "Father give me that share of the estate that would come to me on your death, please". The father granted the son his wish, and soon afterwards the young man left home and departed for a distant country, where he then proceeded to squander his fortune on a very extravagant style of living. Quite soon, all his money was gone, and his circumstances were so reduced that he was happy to take work as a hired hand feeding pigs. Eventually things become so bad that he said to himself, "Even my father's servants have more to eat than I do! I will return home again and throw myself upon my father's mercy saying, father I have sinned against God and you, and though I can no longer expect to be treated as your son, I beg that you allow me to work for you as a hired hand?"

'On the day that he actually reached home, his father was standing at the gate, and seeing the bedraggled and tattered figure approaching, he at first took it to be a beggar. However as soon as he realised that this impoverished creature was his beloved son, the old man's heart immediately went out to him, and he ran to meet him, throwing his arms around his shoulders, and weeping for joy.

'As the son was being led into the house, he said, "Father, I have sinned against God and you, and am therefore no longer worthy to be called your son". Ignoring what he said, the father at once told servants to go quickly and bring the best clothes and shoes in the house for his son to put on. He also ordered that his best fatted calf be slaughtered, and a feast be prepared in his son's honour, saying, "Tonight we shall celebrate, for the son who was lost to me and feared dead, is returned home alive and well".

'In the evening the older son was returning home after a hard day's work in the fields, and hearing the sounds of laughter and music as he approached the house, he asked a servant what was going on. When told what had happened, he was furious, and refused to enter the house. The father came out to plead with him, and begged him not to make an enemy of his brother. The older son replied, "Father, all my life I have honoured you and obeyed your every wish, and never have I given you cause to make complaint against me, yet in all those years you have never so much as given me a goat that I could give a dinner for my fiends. But today your younger son comes home after squandering your money on women, wine and high-living, and at once you kill the fatted calf for him! Where is the justice?" Gazing at his son with tender love in his eyes, the old answered, "My son, you have been here with me all of the time; everything I have is yours, but it is only natural a father should wish to celebrate the return of his long lost son. After all, I thought he might be dead—but he is alive and I rejoice! He was lost, but now he is home again".'

Then Jesus told another story, this time especially for his disciples. 'There was once a rich man who employed a steward to deal with his affairs. One day he received information that the steward had been mishandling things, and the rich man immediately dismissed him. "What am I going to do now?" wailed the steward, "for I have no other clients, and I am not physically suited to work of a manual nature, and I could never bring myself to beg in the streets". Then an idea struck him, and he called in the debtors of his former employer (as if still working for the man), and said to them, "Now let me see, you owe my master for one hundred measures of oil...tear up the old bill, and make out a new one for fifty". Then to another debtor he said, "You owe for one hundred measures of wheat; make it fourscore". Then, quite regardless of his previous condemnation of the steward, the rich man was forced to admire the man's rascally cunning, and promptly reinstated him again.

'Worldly men are often a good deal wiser than good men,' said Jesus, 'and I therefore suggest that money, tainted though it may be, if used wisely can attract those able to be of service to yourself and your aims. The man who is wise in small matters, will be even wiser in important issues. No one can work for two employers; he is bound to favour one more than the other. You cannot serve both Almighty God, and Mammon.'

There were some Pharisees among the people gathered around Jesus as he spoke, and since they were so covetous in money matters, they sneered at these last remarks. Jesus, noticing this, directed his next comments especially at them.

'You Pharisees may make a great show of your piety,' he said, 'but God knows what is in your hearts. The things which inspire men, make not the slightest impact on God. Until the birth of John the Baptist, the Mosaic laws and the sayings of the prophets were the standards on which men based their lives. But John opened the eyes of the people in a way never done before. He brought the good news of God's kingdom and showed the heights to which men can aspire. But in no way did he attempt to change any of God's basic laws; they remain, and must remain law for ever. For instance it remains true that anyone who re-marries after a divorce becomes an adulterer. So is the man who marries a divorced woman.'

Then Jesus told another parable: 'There was once a very rich man who possessed everything that money could buy, beautiful house, with splendid furnishings, the finest clothes, and the best of foods and wines. One day a beggar named Lazarus came and sat at the gates of h is fine house. Covered with running sores and starving with hunger, the poor man longed for a few crumbs from the rich man's table. But though even the dogs had pity on him, and came to lick his sores, the rich man completely ignored him, so that eventually the poor beggar died of hunger. Then it was however, that the poor man 's spirit was elevated to the same sphere as that occupied by Abraham and all the great prophets. When the rich man died and passed to spirit, he discovered that he had been allotted a place in the sphere commonly termed 'Hades'. Suffering great heat and torment, he looked up and far away saw Lazarus walking in perfect peace and comfort by the side of Abraham.

'Father Abraham,' shouted the rich man, 'Please have mercy upon me, and send Lazarus to dip his finger in water that he may come and cool my tongue, for I am in agony amid these flames'. Abraham answered saying, 'Have you forgotten that when you inhabited the material world, you had the very best of everything, and Lazarus had nothing? Now in the spirit world the positions have been reversed, and I must tell you that there is an unbridgable gulf between you; even if Lazarus wished to come to you, it would not be possible'. In despair the rich man cried out, 'Father Abraham, then I beseech you to send Lazarus to my family home, there to warn my five brothers about this terrible place, and so avoid coming here'. Abraham replied, 'They have the teachings of Moses and the prophets and these should be warnings enough'. Then said the rich man, 'I realize this, but if the spirit of a dead man were to appear before them, then this would ensure their repentance'. Unmoved by the pleadings of the rich man, Abraham said, 'If they choose to ignore Moses and the prophets, then they are not likely to take notice of a "dead" man!'

Realising that the parable had been directed at them, the Pharisees said to Jesus, 'Master, help us to attain greater faith.'

'Greater faith?' retorted Jesus, 'Why, if your faith were no larger than a grain of mustard seed, you would be able to say to this mulberry tree standing here, 'Move and cast yourself into the ocean', and it would do it. Let me put a question to you; if you had a servant whose job it was to tend the sheep and plough your fields, would you at the end of the day say to him, "Come in and enjoy the evening meal I have prepared for you" . Is it not more likely that you would say to him, "Now prepare my meal, then change your clothes and serve it to me"

. Do you thank a servant for what he is paid to do? Likewise, should a servant think himself unexceptional if he performs more than his duties call for.'

One day Jesus received an urgent message from the sisters Martha and Mary, in Bethany. The message told that their beloved brother Lazarus, a great friend of Jesus, was desperately ill, and begged that Jesus come to him at all speed. On receipt of the message however, Jesus showed not the slightest need for concern, saying, 'His illness is not of a terminal nature: its purpose is to demonstrate yet again the powers of Almighty God, and thus bring glory upon His son.' Nevertheless, knowing how fond Jesus was of this particular family, the disciples could not help expressing their surprise when he decided to stay where he was for a further two days, and said, 'We are going to Judaea.'

'Master,' they said, 'Only a few days ago the Jews were ready to stone you in Judaea. Do you think it wise to return there so soon?' Jesus answered, 'There are twelve hours in each day, are there not? One does not stumble during the day because there is light to see, only at night in the dark does one stumble.' Then pausing for a moment's meditation, he said, 'Our friend Lazarus has merely fallen asleep, but I must go and awaken him.'

'But Master,' said the disciples, 'if he has only fallen asleep, then there is no danger.' Bluntly Jesus replied, 'Lazarus is dead. Now yet again am I afforded an opportunity to strengthen your wilting faith. Let us be on our way.'

By the time they actually reached Bethany, Lazarus had been buried four days. As Jesus and his followers drew near to the house, word went ahead that he was on his way, and Martha ran out to meet him. 'Oh Master,' the poor woman cried, tears running down her face, 'if only you had come when first we sent our message, Lazarus would still be alive. Even now though, as late as it is, I know that God will grant whatever you ask.'

Putting an arm around her shoulders and with great gentleness, Jesus said, 'Your brother will rise again, Martha.' Sadly, she said, 'Oh I know he will rise again in the world of spirits, but that is not what I had hoped for.'

Tenderly Jesus said, 'Martha, I am the resurrection of life, and he who believes in me shall live for ever. Do you believe this?'

Yes,' she said. 'I believe you are the Christ—God's promised one, for whom we have been waiting.' Then running home ahead of him, she told Mary 'The Master is here, and he wants to see you.' Jumping to her feet Mary therefore hastened to meet him, and all the mourners, seeing her depart so hastily, followed quickly at her heels. Falling at the feet of Jesus, Mary sobbed bitterly, 'Oh Master, if only you had been here, Lazarus would not now be dead.'

Moved with great pity and compassion, Jesus put a hand gently on Mary's head and asked, 'Where is he buried?'

'Come,' said Mary, 'I will show you.' Suddenly Jesus himself burst into tears, and one of the mourners was heard to remark, 'See how much he loved his friend Lazarus,' but another countered saying, 'If he has the power to open the eyes of the blind, could he not have kept Lazarus from death?'

Reaching the cave that served as a tomb for Lazarus, Jesus asked that the great stone covering the entrance to the cave be rolled away. 'You cannot go in there!' Martha cried. 'He has been dead for four days, and the stench will be terrible.'

'My child, did I not say to you, trust in God, and his glory will be revealed to you?' replied Jesus. The stone having been removed, he then knelt before the entrance, and lifting his eyes heaven-wards said, 'Father, I give thanks that thou has always heard me in the past. I know you always do, and I say it now only so that those gathered about me may know I am here because *you* sent me.'

Then, concentrating the full force of his psychic powers, he called out, 'Lazarus, come forth!' Everyone stood around the entrance to the cave not knowing quite what to expect, and a gasp of astonishment went up as Lazarus, wrapped from head to foot in his burial clothes, came slowly out of the darkness, into the light. With tears of joy streaming down their faces, Martha and Mary immediately rushed forward to embrace him, and as they did so, Jesus said 'Remove the bindings and take him home.'

In no time at all, news of what had happened in Bethany spread far and wide; everyone was excitedly talking about the way Jesus had raised Lazarus from the dead. When the Pharisees in Jerusalem heard about it, they hurriedly held a council meeting to discuss what should be done.

'It has to be admitted that this men Jesus does accomplish the most amazing things,' they said, 'but if he is allowed to continue like this, his popularity with the people will create trouble, both for us, and our Roman masters; they will see him as a threat to public order, and a challenge to their authority. He must not be allowed to destroy our society.'

'I agree', shouted Caiaphas, the high priest. ' It would be better for one man to die for the people, than that a whole nation be destroyed.' The council, being unanimous in its opinions, laid plans as to the best way to arrest Jesus and have him executed.

Thus it was that Caiaphas, without realising it, came to predict that Jesus would die, not just for the sake of Israel, but to bring together all the dispersed children of God as one united family.

Knowing the intention of the priests, Jesus and his followers removed to a village on the edge of the desert, where he might have time and peace to pray and meditate on the last phase of his earthly life.

## 30

*Jesus discusses the laws of Moses*

Soon Jesus and his followers set out for Jerusalem again. The disciples wondering why, in the face of the hostility and hatred that awaited him, he should risk venturing there, but realising he must have some plan to fulfil.

They had not gone far, when ten Lepers suddenly appeared before them, and standing some way off they called out, 'Jesus of Nazareth, we have heard about your miracles of healing, please help us.'

'Go show yourselves to the priests,' Jesus called out, and as they hurried off to do so, they suddenly became aware that the dreaded Leprosy had left them, and they were completely cleansed and healthy again. Great was their rejoicing, buy only one, a Samaritan, thought of going back to thank Jesus for his efforts on their behalf.

Having found Jesus on the road, the Samaritan fell at Jesus's feet, praising and glorifying God for his recovery. Looking down at the men, Jesus said, 'Were there not ten of you? Where are the others? Are you the only one who thanks God for what he has done?'

A group of Pharisees were standing nearby at the time, and one of them said to Jesus, 'When do you say the Kingdom of Heaven will come?' He replied, 'If you mean in a visible form, then the answer is never. People will not be able to say, "It is here— it is there', because the Kingdom of Heaven is in your very midst."

Then turning to his followers he said, ' The time is soon coming when I shall no longer be among you. Rumours will spread that I have been seen here, or seen there, but you must take no notice of them. When I do return, it shall be like a bolt of lightning that lights the sky from horizon to horizon...all will be aware.' Then in a quieter and more contemplative mood he added, 'But before that time comes, I have much suffering to experience, and even the rejection of those I have come to save.'

Then, wishing to impress on his followers the need for prayers and meditation as the best way to combat waning enthusiasm, Jesus told them a little story: 'Once there was a judge who had nothing to fear from neither God nor man, so fair were the judgements he gave. But the time came when a certain woman became a great nuisance to him, constantly complaining about a certain wrong that had been done to her, and insisting that he do something to remedy the matter. At first the judge refused to get involved, but in time he grew weary of her constant hounding of him and said, "I had better do something for her, or she will drive me mad with her unending pleadings".' Then Jesus said to his followers, 'Note the judge's reaction. Likewise you may rest assured that constant prayers do not go unheeded.'

Next Jesus related a story about people who continually congratulated themselves on their good virtues, but looked down on other people around them: 'Two men went up to the temple to pray. One was a greatly respected Pharisee, the other a despised tax-collector. In his prayer to God, the Pharisee said, "Dear God, how grateful am I that I am not like other men...greedy, unprincipled and immoral...unlike that tax-collector over there. Twice a week I fast, and from all the money I earn, one tenth I give to the temple." A short distance away, but in the shadows because he felt himself to be so unworthy, the tax-collector struck himself on the chest, and lifting his eyes towards heaven said, "Dear God, please have mercy on me, as sinful and unworthy as I am."

Then looking round at his followers Jesus commented, 'You may be sure than when those two men left the temple, it was the tax-collector and not the Pharisee who caught the ear of God. All those who place themselves upon a pedestal shall be torn down, while the meek and the humble shall receive all honour.'

Continuing his journey to Jerusalem, Jesus constantly stopped at small villages and towns on the way, to teach the crowds of people who turned out to see him, and also heal the sick. At one such place a group of Pharisees put a question to him, their true purpose being to ensnare him. 'Are there any grounds on which a man may divorce his wife?' they asked.

'What says the law of Moses?' asked Jesus.

One of the Pharisees spoke up, 'He says it is permitted so long as the wife is given a divorce certificate.'

Then Jesus said, 'The reason Moses permitted such a thing was because you are so lacking in love for each other. Cast back your mind to the story of the creation; it states that God made man and woman and commanded that *for this reason a man shall leave his parents and stay with his wife, and the two of them shall be as ONE person.* A married couple is a unit, and no one should separate those whom God has joined.'

Later that same day when Jesus was talking with his followers, one of them revived the question of Moses and the divorce certificate, saying, 'Master, if what you told the Pharisee was true, why did Moses allow men to leave their wives after supplying such a document?'

'Because at that particular time it was expedient to do so, and because men were so lacking in love,' Jesus answered. 'However that is not the way things were in the beginning, and God's law is quite clear on the matter. Any man who divorces his wife for any other reason than that she has been unfaithful, and marries again, becomes an adulterer. The same applies to any man who marries a divorced woman. Also, if a woman divorces her husband and remarries, then she too commits adultery.'

One young follower spoke out saying, 'Well if that's how it is, surely it is better not to get married at all.'

'No one suggests that it is an easy teaching to accept,' said Jesus, adding, 'it takes a special kind of man. There are men who are eunuchs because they were born so, others have been made so, and there are men who are purposely continent for the sake of attaining a higher place in heaven. If you have the will-power to follow my teachings, then the better for you.'

A few days later, as Jesus entered a village, some women came towards him with their children, it being their desire that he should touch the little ones, and say a prayer for them. However, the disciples considering them a nuisance, attempted to keep them away from him. Seeing this, Jesus became angry and called out, 'Let the little ones come to me, how dare you attempt to stop them. They are what the Kingdom of Heaven is all about. The truth is that he who does not accept the kingdom with the simplicity of one of these little ones, shall never enter it.' Then, walking among the children and placing his hands upon them, he gave them his blessing.

Later as Jesus walked through the village, a young man who was a ruler in the Jewish quarter, ran up to him and said, 'good Sir, what should I do to inherit eternal life?'

'Why do you call me good?' asked Jesus, 'Only God is good. What must you do? Well you are aware of God's commandments: do not kill, do not commit adultery, do not steal, do not lie, honour your father and your mother, and have as much regard for your neighbour as you have for yourself. Keep these commandments.'

The young man replied, 'All these have I kept since I was a boy, but what else must I do? '

Jesus answered, 'If you would be perfect and follow me, then must you sell all your earthly possessions and give the proceeds to the poor. Do this, and you shall build up treasures for yourself in heaven.'

Hearing this, the youth walked slowly away looking extremely downcast, for he was a young man of great wealth. As he departed, Jesus turned to his disciples and said, 'It is easier for a camel to pass through the eye of a needle, than for a rich man to enter the Kingdom of God.'

Then said Peter to Jesus, 'What of us who have forsaken all to follow thee?' He answered, 'When I sit upon my throne in glory, you shall sit upon twelve thrones, judging the twelve tribes of Israel, and all who have faithfully obeyed the laws and followed all my teachings, shall be elevated to that place of eternal bliss and harmony which the Kingdom of Heaven. In the spirit world all men shall be judged by their earthly conduct, and a great and mighty king may find himself reduced to the role of a beggar, while a humble beggar could find himself transported to a position among the prophets and chosen one of old.'

As Jesus and his large party of followers drew nearer to Jerusalem, he called the chosen twelve to his side and said to them, ' Understand that this present journey to Jerusalem is to fulfil the predictions of the prophets of old. I shall, as foretold, be betrayed and handed over to the chief priests and scribes, who shall condemn me to death, and hand me over to the Romans, who will make sport of me, shall flog and crucify me. But on the third day, I shall rise again.'

Continuing his journey with his followers, Jesus arrived at the City of Jericho. Here dense crowds who had heard of his coming, turned out into the streets to get a glimpse of him. One such person was Zacchaeus, a chief tax-collector, and a man of great wealth. Short in stature, Zacchaeus had taken up a position in one of the streets hoping to see Jesus pass, but unable to see over the shoulders of the people in front of him, he climbed a nearby Sycamore tree, to gain a better view. As Jesus passed by, he looked up into the tree and called out, 'Come down Zacchaeus, I wish to avail myself of your hospitality this day.' Zacchaeus scrambled down at one and, delighted at having the opportunity of entertaining such a well known figure, led the way to his home. Many spectators were outraged: 'Imagine Jesus seeking hospitality with that scoundrel,' they said.

Later, after Jesus and many of his followers had been lodged most comfortably by Zacchaeus, and provided with ample food and drink, he said to Jesus, 'Teacher, I have decided to give half of everything I own to the poor and needy, and where I have defrauded any tax-payer, I intend to repay the amount four times over.'

Jesus, delighted that his visit to Zacchaeus had culminated in such a happy ending, said to him, 'This day has salvation come upon this house. I came to seek and save the lost, and this day Zacchaeus has proved that he is a son of Abraham also.'

Jesus was aware that his followers, though equally impressed by the generosity of Zacchaeus, still could not comprehend the Kingdom of Heaven, some of them persisting in the notion that it would be an earthly domain that would be set up when Jesus reached Jerusalem. He therefore decided to tell them another of his parables:

'A certain nobleman needed to visit a distant country where he had been given a kingdom. Before leaving, he called ten of his servants together and to each of them gave a sum of money, saying, "I wish you to invest this while I am away." When he eventually returned home again, he sent for each of the servants in turn, and asked them to give an account of what they had done with the money. The first said, "Sir, your money has earned ten times its value." The nobleman was pleased. "good," he said, "You are an excellent servant, and now that you have shown how well you can handle a simple task, you shall take charge of ten cities in the kingdom which has recently become mine." The second servant came to him and said, "Sir, I invested you money and it has earned five times its original value."

"Splendid," said the nobleman, "You shall rule five cities in my new kingdom." Another servant came forward and, handing over the exact sum of money that had been deposited with him, said "Sir, knowing you to be a very austere man who reaps from others what he has not sown himself, and who derives much pleasure and gain from the toil and sweat of others, I was fearful, and decided simply to keep your money safe until your return."

"You wretch" shouted the nobleman, "You shall be judged out of your own mouth. If, as you say, you know the kind of man I am, why then did you not at least invest the money in a bank where it could gain some interest?" Then he ordered another servant to take the money from the third servant and give it to the first. "But he already has a great amount of money," said the others. "This may be so," said the nobleman, "but I say that those who already have, are going to receive more, and those who have nothing, shall be given nothing".' The story ended, Jesus retired for the night.

Next morning when Jesus and his followers were leaving Jericho, they passed two blind beggars on the outskirts of the city. Sitting together at the roadside and hearing the sounds of a large crowd approaching, one of them, whose name was Bartimaeus, asked what was happening. 'Jesus of Nazareth and a large group of his followers are passing by,' someone told him.

'Jesus of Nazareth here?' he exclaimed, and at once he started shouting as loudly as he could, 'Jesus! Jesus son of David! Have mercy on me!'

'Be quiet,' called someone. 'Hold your peace,' said another. But stop he would not, indeed he only shouted all the louder, 'Jesus have pity on us!' he yelled.

Hearing the desperate cries for help, Jesus stopped; and as he did so, the large throng following him also halted, ceasing in their idle chatter. 'Bring the beggar to me,' Jesus said. Almost before he could be invited to come forward, Bartimaeus leapt to his feet and started to stumble towards Jesus, the other beggar following hot on his heels.

'What would you have me do?' asked Jesus.

'Please, Master. Give us our sight,' begged Bartimaeus.

Filled with love and compassion, and deeply moved that Bartimaeus had such faith in his powers, Jesus said, 'Your sight be restored. Your faith has healed you.' Immediately both beggars gave a great gasp of delight, realizing that their wishes had been granted. They threw themselves down into the dust at Jesus's feet, but already he had started to move again, so they followed after him, praising God on high as they went.

# 31

## *Jesus arrives in Jerusalem*

With still six days to go the Festival of the Passover, Jesus and his followers arrived in Bethany, making their way to the home of Lazarus, and his sisters Martha and Mary. News of his arrival spread rapidly through the village, and soon people came in great numbers to catch a glimpse of this great prophet who had brought Lazarus back from the dead.

Jesus rested at the home of Lazarus a few days, then on the Sunday began the last stage of his journey to Jerusalem. Outside the city however, on the slope of the Mount of Olives and close by the village of Bethphage, Jesus called two of his followers to him, saying, 'Go to yonder village, and as soon as you enter it you will find a donkey with an unbroken colt beside it, tethered to a post. Bring the animals to me, and if anyone asks what you are doing, answer that the teacher has need of them. You will have no trouble.'

Going into the village as instructed, they found the donkey and colt, exactly as Jesus had foretold. As they were loosing the halter, the owner of the animals came up and asked them what they were doing. When they answered 'The teacher needs them,' the man said no more and they lead the animals away.

Having brought the animals to Jesus, the disciples spread a cloak over the back of the colt and Jesus mounted it. At the time his followers thought little of these simple occurrences, but later they came to realise that they had helped to fulfil yet one more prophecy from the Scriptures:

> Tell this to our daughter, Zion;
> Have no fear, your king approaches,
> Meek, and mounted on an ass;

Upon a colt, the foal of an ass.

Jerusalem was by now overflowing with many thousands of people who had poured into the city from all over the country for celebration of the Passover, and amongst these Jesus was the chief topic of conversation. Citizens and pilgrims alike wondering whether he would dare to show his face in the city, it being common knowledge that the council of priests were anxious to arrest him. The priests knew that if Jesus succeeded in convincing the people of his doctrines, their whole system would be overthrown and the fat living they extracted from the ignorant masses would be at an end.

As Jesus approached Jerusalem, he found the road was lined with great crowds who were consumed with both awe and curiosity. Some people who had been into nearby fields and cut branches of Palm, strewed these in his path. Others spread their cloaks in the road for him to ride over, and the air was filled with cries of jubilation.

'Praise for the king who comes in God's holy name!' they shouted. 'Save us blessed Jesus! Deliver us O king of Israel! blessed be thy coming kingdom! '

Deeply concerned by this frenzied display of adulation, a group of Pharisees called out to Jesus, 'Teacher, tell your followers to stop all this.'

'Tell them to stop?' he called back, 'Why, where I to try, the very stones themselves would cry out.'

Approaching the gate of the city, Jesus became very solemn, and tears began to fill his eyes. 'Oh Jerusalem,' he said, 'If only you had been aware on what your peace depends. If only you had seized your God-given opportunity. Now it is hidden from your eyes, but the time approaches when an enemy shall surround you walls and tear them down, slaughter your citizens, and leave no stone standing upon another.'

Wending his way through the narrow streets of the city, on all sides the excited crowds greeted him, even little children copied their parents, shouting, 'Deliver us, son of David!' The Pharisees seethed with anger at his popularity, and called out, 'Do you hear what even the children call you?'

'Yes, I hear them,' shouted Jesus, 'and does not the scripture say, *from the lips of infants, God has proved perfect praise.'*

Jesus's destination was the temple, and on arrival there, he found the usual collection of traders and money-lenders doing business. Walking round the temple enclosure in a violent rage, he overturned their tables and stands, forbidding anyone to carry so much as even a water jug through the enclosure. 'Hasn't it been written,' he demanded, *'My house shall be known as a place where all may pray?* You people have turned it into a haven for thieves!'

Eager as were the council of priests to have Jesus arrested, his current popularity and public adulation made it clear that they must proceed with caution, and they therefore deferred plans until they could discuss the matter further.

In the meantime Jesus went daily to the temple, teaching the large assembly of people who gathered there to hear him. In the evenings he and his followers went to the garden in Kedron, where they found shelter, and though under the open canopy of heaven they were at least away from the noise and bustle of the city.

One evening as Jesus sat in the gardens with his followers, he said, 'The time fast approaches when I am to be glorified. As you already know, a grain of wheat will not produce more wheat unless it first "dies" and is buried in the soil. That is why I have said so often that to love life is to lose it; while to "die" is to keep it for ever. If you truly wish to serve me and follow me in all things, then will my Father honour you, and you shall be with me always.

'Now that my time draws near, I must confess my spirit grows troubled with the thoughts of what lies ahead of me—yet why should this be, for was this not my very purpose in coming. Should I shrink from by chosen course, saying, "Father save me from this"...No! rather must I say, " Father, glorify thy name".'

As Jesus spoke these words, a voice was clearly heard to say, 'As I have done in the past, so shall I do in the future.'

His followers gazed at each other in wonder, and as they did so Jesus said, 'The voice spoke more for your benefit than mine. This is a time of judgment for mankind, for misguided leaders are going to reject their own creator, but when I, the son of man am risen from my material shell, then shall the whole world be drawn to me, and through me to be re-united with the Father.' So saying, Jesus wandered off alone to a part of the gardens where he might pray and meditate on what lay before him.

On the following day, as Jesus made his way back to the city, he felt hungry, and seeing a fig-tree near the roadside, went to it hoping to find fruit. Alas it had leaves only, and Jesus said to his followers, 'How like unto the Jews of Jerusalem is this tree. It's appearance gives hope to the hungry, but examination only proves that it is quite devoid of that which could sustain life. So with the temple in Jerusalem which should offer hope to the spiritually hungry, but on examination offers nothing but the gilded glory of a soulless, useless religion.'

Then Jesus said, 'Henceforth let there be no fruit from this tree ever again,' and instantly the fig-tree began to wither away. Marvelling at this remarkable sight, his followers asked how he had accomplished such a thing. He told them it was the result of prayer with conviction and that such psychic power lay within each one of them. All that was needed was the stimulus of true faith to set the action going.

On reaching the temple, Jesus began to address the people gathered there, saying, 'When you believe in me, you are not so much believing in me as in the Father who sent me. To see me, is to see him, I am the light, and when you believe in me you no longer live in darkness. If any man hears my words but believes me not, I shall not pass judgment on him, for I came not to judge the world, but to save it. You shall however be judged by my teachings, for the things I teach are not my thoughts, but God's. What I say, he has commanded. When you hear me speak, the voice may be mine, but the words are God's.'

As Jesus was speaking to the people, a delegation of the temple priests and elders came up saying, 'We demand to know on whose authority you act.'

'Answer my question,' replied Jesus, 'and I will answer yours: John the Baptist's ministry was it of God, or merely the action of a man?'

Drawing aside, the priests and elders conferred with each other: 'If we say John was from God, then Jesus will ask why we refuse to believe what John said about him. On the other hand, if we say that John did not come from God, then there will be trouble with the people, for they are convinced that John was a prophet—why they might even stone us.'

Going back to Jesus they said, 'We do not know which it was.'

'You mean you refuse to say,' said Jesus. 'Very well, then neither will I say who gave me my authority.'

Then Jesus told them a parable: 'A man has two sons. Going to the first son the father says, "I wish you to work in the vineyard today." At first the son refuses, but later changes his mind and goes. Then the father goes to his second son, and makes the same request. The son answers, 'Very well father, I will go', but in fact he does not. Now answer me this—which son did what his father wanted?'

The priests and elders answered, 'Why the first of course.'

Then Jesus said, 'Well, let it be understood that whores and thieves shall be admitted to the kingdom before you. You refused to accept the words of John the Baptist, but outcasts did. '

Then Jesus gave they yet another parable: 'A certain man, having planted a vineyard, put a hedge round it, dug a pit for a winepress and built a watchtower for protection. The work completed, he decided to reside in another country, leasing out this property. At the appropriate time the man sent one of his servants to collect the payments due. However when the servant arrived on the errand for his master, the tenants beat him severely and sent him away empty handed. A second servant was sent, this man the tenants stoned and also drove away. When a third servant was sent to them, they killed him. By now the owner of the property had grown very frustrated, and said to himself, "I know, I will send by own son to them, at least they will have proper respect for him." But when the tenants saw the young man approaching, they said, "Look, here comes the heir to the estate. Let us kill him, then his legacy will be ours." Having murdered him, they buried the body off the property.

'Now I put this question to you,' said Jesus 'What would the owner of the property do to such men as these? I will tell you what he would do: he would destroy the miserable wretches, and lease the vineyard to others who will render what is due.

'Do not the scriptures clearly indicate, *the stone the builders reject has become a cornerstone.'* Then pointing an accusing finger at the priests and elders, Jesus added, 'Indeed shall the Kingdom of God be taken away from the likes of you, and given to people who will yield a proper return.'

Smouldering with anger that Jesus should so publicly humiliate them, the priests and elders departed from the temple enclosure, smarting under the verbal wounds he had inflicted upon them. More than ever they were determined to destroy him now, but still they hesitated to arrest him, his popularity being such that they feared the reaction of the public.

A group of Pharisees, witnessing how the priests had been rebuked, decided to see how they might fare putting a question to Jesus. 'Teacher,' they said, 'we know you to be an honest man, a man not to be influenced by what others might do or say, so tell us truthfully—is it right to pay taxes to Caesar or not?'

Aware that their real intention was to embroil him with the Roman authorities, Jesus cried out, 'You hypocrites! Why do you attempt to trap me thus?' Then asking one of the Pharisees for a coin, Jesus held it up before them and said, 'Whose name and image do you see on this coin?'

'Caesar's,' they answered.

'Then give to Caesar what is his, and to God what is God's' Jesus said. Knowing full well that there was no further argument to be made, the Pharisees slowly walked away, very impressed by his simple answer.

Next a group of Sadducees put a question to Jesus. 'Teacher,' said their spokesman, 'We are told by Moses that if a man dies without heir, his brother is required to marry the widow and raise a family for him. Now say there were seven brothers, and the eldest dies leaving a widow but no children. The second brother marries her, but also dies childless. The third brother does the same, so in turn do all the others, until eventually the woman herself dies. Our question is this: when all seven brothers and the woman are resurrected, whose wife will she be?'

Jesus answered, 'Because you do not understand either the scriptures or the power of God, you are confused. Only in the material world do men and women marry. Marriage, like sex, does not exist in the spirit world—all being equally God's children.'

'Well answered, Teacher!' said an old man in the crowd 'Now would you be good enough to explain something for me? Which is the most important of all the commandments?'

Jesus replied, 'That commandment which goes, "Listen Israel: the Lord our God is the only God. You shall love him with all that you are—your will, your spirit, your intellect and your body." That is the first and most important. The second commandment is akin to it: "You shall have as much regard for your neighbour as for yourself." No other commandments are as important as these, and everything in the law and the prophets is predicted on them.'

'Agreed, Teacher,' said the old man 'How much better to love God and one's neighbours than to offer useless sacrifices and burnt offerings on an altar.'

Delighted by the old man's remark, and realising that here was someone with deep insight, Jesus said, ' Your pathway leads straight to the kingdom my brother.'

There now being a break in the questioning, Jesus decided to put a question of his own to a group of Pharisees still standing there. 'Let me ask your views on the Messiah,' he said 'Who do you say he is descended from?'

'Why, he will be descended from king David of course,' said one of them.

Then Jesus said, 'That being so, how do you account for the fact that David, when speaking under God's inspiration said, *the Lord said to my Lord: sit here at my right until I put your enemies under foot.'* Would David have called the Messiah "Lord" if he were his son?'

Since the Pharisees offered no reply, Jesus turned to his disciples and said in a loud clear voice so that all might hear, 'Be warned about the scribes and Pharisees. They have the authority of Moses invested in them, so do what they say. But do not do as they do, for they practise not what they preach. They heap heavy burdens on the backs of the people, but do not lift a finger to help them. Even the worthwhile things that they do are spoilt by their false piety. How they love the outward show, enlarging their phylacteries, lengthening the tassels on their robes. How they love to occupy the front seats in the synagogue, and how they enjoy being addressed as "Rabbi". But you should let no one call you "Rabbi"; only one is your teacher, the rest of you are brothers in equality. Neither must you address anyone here on earth as "Father'—you have only one father, and He is in heaven. Nor must you refer to yourself as "Master'—for there is only one master, and he is the Christ.'

Then addressing himself pointedly to the Pharisees in his audience, Jesus, 'Woe unto you scribes and Pharisees, you hypocrites and blind guides. Not only do you ban yourselves from heaven, but you persuade others to follow your example. You go to great lengths to make a convert and, having done so, only produce a devil twice as vile as yourselves. You tell the man who swears an oath by the temple that it isn't binding, whereas the man who swears by the temple gold that it is! You say that if a man swears on oath by the altar it means nothing, yet if he swears by the gift on the altar the it is binding! what kind of logic is this? Which is the more important; the gold, or the temple that makes the gold sacred? If you swear by the altar, you swear by the altar and anything on it. If you swear by the temple, you swear by the temple and the God who dwells therein. If you swear by heaven, then you swear by God's throne and by God Himself. You wretched scribes and Pharisees; so precise about the smallest obligation to the temple, yet so neglectful of the basic laws, particularly those dealing with justice, compassion, and faith. Understand I find no fault in what you do, only in what you do not do—the things that really matter. Your leaders are so blind, and so busy looking for a gnat in your drink, that they fail to see the camel floating there. You vile hypocrites;— cease scrubbing the surfaces of your cups and plates, and pay attention to the filth—the greed and rapacity that lies within you. Get your priorities right. Alas, you are like whitewashed tombs—attractive on the outside, but filled with bones and stinking corruption inside. To the outside world you may appear Godly men, but in truth you are filled with hypocrisy and evil.

'You build monuments to the prophets to honour them, yet at the same time in your minds you are thinking, "Had we but lived in the time of these people, we would have joined with our ancestors in murdering them". You are indeed descendants of the men who murdered the prophets. You brood of snakes! I realise that though I send learned men and prophets to you, like your ancestors you will murder some and crucify others. Some you will drag from the synagogues and flog, others you will hound from town to town. In so doing you shall share in the guilt of spilling the blood of every good man ever put to death: from the blood of the innocent Abel until the present. Be sure this generation, and your children after you, shall answer for it all!

'Oh Jerusalem. How many prophets have you murdered? How many of God's messengers have you stoned? Many are the times I have wished to draw your citizens to me as a mother hen might gather a brood of chicks under her protecting wings, but you would have none of it. Now you shall be left to face the consequences. No more shall you see me again, until your citizens unite in the cry, "Here is the blessed One, the Lord's Ambassador".'

Indicating that his teaching was at an end, the crowd began to disperse, and Jesus sat down in the temple enclosure opposite the Treasury. As he watched, a continual stream of people came, dropping offerings of money into the coffers. Some of the people were wealthy, and the donations they made large, then Jesus noticed a poor poverty-stricken widow drop just two small coins into the boxes. Turning to his disciples Jesus said, 'See, that poor widow has given far more than all the rest. For while they have given of their surplus, that poor woman gave everything she had, leaving herself not even enough to live on.'

As Jesus was leaving the temple, one of his followers commented on the splendour of the masonry on the temple buildings. Jesus said, 'The time is coming when every one of these buildings will be destroyed—there will not be one stone standing upon another.'

Later, when Jesus and his followers were resting on the Mount of Olives, one of them said to him, 'Master, earlier you said the temple was going to be destroyed. Tell us when, and tell us also how we shall know when you intend to return to us again, and when the world itself is to come to an end.'

Jesus answered, 'First lest me warn you (future generations), to be on your guard against those who would lead you astray, for there will be many impostors claiming to be the Messiah, and many are the people who will be fooled. Some of these impostors will even claim to be acting with my authority, and will announce that the end-time is near. Ignore them. There will be many wars, many famines and catastrophes, but these will have nothing to do with the end-time. The time will come when my supporters everywhere will be persecuted, some will be killed, and many will desert me. Some will betray their friends, brothers shall grow to hate each other, and self-proclaimed prophets will draw many to them. The moral standards of society throughout the world will degenerate, and evil flourish. But those who stay faithful to me through such times, shall see the fully glory of heaven.

'The end shall not come until such time as every country of the world has been given the good news of my coming, has had time to understand it, and freely has made a choice between good or evil. Then shall God's vengeance descend upon the earth, and the evil ones shall find no escape. It shall be a time such as no other in the history of the world. The sun shall grow dim, the moon shall not be visible at all, and entire nations shall panic as they realise the end is about to break upon them. Then suddenly amid all the terror and destruction that shall take place, the bright beams of salvation shall burst forth through all the darkness, and only those who have been true to me shall survive.

'When the sap returns to the fig-tree and fresh shoots begin to appear, you do not need to be told that summer is on the way. Likewise when the things I have been describing start to happen, then you will know that I am about to return.

'As to the precise day or hour when the end-time shall come, I cannot tell you—no one but the Father himself knows this. That being so, you have all the more reason to be vigilant and on your guard, obeying the commandments and showing proper respect for him who is your heavenly Father, for you know not when you shall be called to give account of yourselves.

'Be prepared at all times. For when I judge you, it will be in the same manner that a shepherd separates the sheep from the goats You shall be set apart, the sheep going to my right, the goats to my left. Then shall I say to those on my right

"Come all you whom my Father has loved since the beginning of time. Take the place he has prepared for you in the kingdom. It is yours because when I hungered you fed me, when I thirsted you gave me drink. When I was lonely you welcomed me. When I was naked you clothed me. When I was sick or a prisoner, you visited me and gave me cheer." They will reply, "But when did we do all these things? We do not recall you hungry, thirsty, or without clothes, neither do we remember visiting you when you were sick or in prison." Then shall I say to them, "When you did such things for the least important of your fellow-men, then in effect were you doing it for me."

'Then shall I turn to those on my left saying. "Be off with you, out of my sight and into that sphere best suited for the likes of you. You cared not when I was hungry or thirsty, and you turned away when I was in need of clothes to cover my nakedness. When I was sick, and in prison through no fault of my own, you lifted not a finger to help me." Then they also will say, "But we recall none of these things," and I shall say to them "When you turned your back on the humblest of your fellow-men, then did you turn your back on me." Then shall they be sent off to a place where punishment is never ending.'

Returning to the present, Jesus said to his followers, 'Understand and prepare yourselves, for following the Passover in two days time, I shall be arrested and crucified.'

That evening, accompanied by his followers, Jesus went to Bethany, where Lazarus and Martha had prepared supper for them. Whilst they were sitting at the table, Mary came in carrying an alabaster flask filled with a very expensive perfumed oil. This she then proceeded to sprinkle onto the head and feet of Jesus, filling the whole house with its lovely fragrance.

'What a shocking extravagance,' blurted out Judas Iscariot 'What a waste...the money spent on that perfume should have gone to the poor.' In truth his concern was not so much for the poor, as for himself, since being treasurer of the group and custodian of the purse, he on occasions helped himself to the group's funds.

Several other followers also made critical comment, but Jesus, seeing the hurt expression on Mary's face said, 'Stop criticizing the girl. She has done a beautiful thing. The poor you will always have with you to care for, but I shall be gone from you shortly. It is but a form of anointing me before my burial, and when in the future the glad tidings of my resurrection shall be recounted throughout the world, then will Mary be remembered for this lovely act.'

Shortly after this, Judas slipped away from Bethany and went to the temple in Jerusalem where, after a short discussion with a group of chief priests, he agreed to betray Jesus to them for thirty pieces of silver.

# 32

## *The council of scribes and priests*

When the chief priests and scribes did in fact hold council to discuss how best to deal with Jesus, they found that not all of their number were so ready to condemn him. Now that the storm was about to break, those who were boldly ready to stand up in his defence included Nicodemus, Joseph of Arimathaea, Gamaliel, and several other leaders of Israel.

The high priest Caiaphas, having risen from his great throne, addressed the assembled council. After saying what Jesus had done and was doing, he accused Jesus of being in league with the Devil, and stated that witnesses were ready to declare that he had spoken both against the temple and the city, and that he had despised the laws of Moses—laws that had been given by God himself. Another rose and accused Jesus of making himself king, this giving the Roman government cause to complain, and an excuse for interference; while yet more brought further charges against him, clamouring for an instant decision.

At this point in the proceedings, the humble and meek-minded Gamaliel rose to the defence of Jesus. He asked how it was that such an evil monster as they had declared Jesus to be, could possibly perform so many good and wonderful works unless God were on his side, adding that many witnesses could also be found to verify these feats of goodness.

Shaking with anger, another priest rose and appealed to heaven to crush the meek Gamaliel. However the greatly respected Nicodemus then boldly stood up and quietly but firmly thrust back the accusations that had been made against Jesus. He said he would not call down the curses of heaven on their heads, rather would he plead for mercy on them, bearing in mind the iniquitous courses they had pursued to gain their object—the destruction of the innocent. 'O blessed religion, as taught by Jesus, glittering in the beauty of truth!' he cried. 'But when put on as a cloak, it becomes dark and cruel, seeking to appease offended heaven by sacrifices on bloody altars. This is not the religion taught by Jesus. Why do you thus secretly meet to sit in judgment of him? He is not afraid to look you in the face. Are you afraid? But go on in your evil way, and become guilty of slaying the innocent. Rear your altar you priests! Lead forth as the victim, for the last of your bloody sacrifices, Jesus, the son of the Living God!'

Thus spoke Nicodemus, who had long been a believer in secret, but who now spoke out bravely in defence of Jesus before the chief priests and Rulers of the nation. 'I leave you now,' he said, 'I wash my hands of this evil deed!' On saying which, accompanied by Joseph, Gamaliel and others, he left the council.

Caiaphas, whilst wishing he could summon sufficient courage to do the same, was afraid for his position as high priest. The majority decision being for the arrest and trial of Jesus, Caiaphas issued orders that the temple guard should seize him—but not until the Passover celebrations were over, for fear of public rioting.

## 33

### *The Last Supper*

On the Thursday, the day before Passover began, Peter and John when to Jesus asking if he had any special place in mind for eating the Passover meal. He replied, 'Yes. Go to Jerusalem, and just as you enter the city, your attention will be drawn to a man carrying a pitcher of water. Follow him, and seek the owner of the house you see him enter. Say to him, "Our Master bids us ask where is the room in which he is to eat the Passover meal with his followers?" He will then lead you to a large room upstairs, after which you are to make all the necessary arrangements for the meal.'

That evening, Jesus and a large number of his followers, including all twelve apostles, sat down together in the room. 'How I have looked forward to partaking of this Passover meal with you, before my agonies begin, ' Jesus said, 'and I shall not eat the Passover meal again, until such time as all that it implies has become factual.'

Then, picking up the bread and breaking it in portions to be shared among them, he gave thanks to the Almighty and said, 'This is my body which I give to you; and this,' he said, lifting a cup of wine to his lips, 'is my blood which I shed for you. This way would I have you remember me.' Then passing the cup around the table so that all might drink of it, he added, 'This will seal the new covenant. I will not drink wine again until we are all come together in the new kingdom.'

At the mention of the new kingdom, several of the apostles began to argue amongst themselves who would be the more prominent in this new domain. Calling for silence, Jesus said, 'Have you learned nothing? Has all my teaching been in vain? How many times must I tell you that each should seek to be the servant of the others, and not the master. Tell me, who is the more important, the man sitting at the table, or the man serving? Surely it is the man being served? Yet here we are, and I am your servant. You have kept faith with me through all my various trials, and in due time each of you shall be rewarded by being made judges of the twelve Tribes of Israel.'

Now, fully aware that this was to be his last night on earth, Jesus rose from the table and, taking off his outer robe, proceeded to tie a towel round his waist. Then, after pouring some water into a basin, he began to wash the feet of the disciples afterwards drying them with the towel.

When, however, he came to Peter, the disciple said, 'Are you going to wash my feet also? It is not fitting that you, our Master should perform such a lowly service...you shall not wash mine!'

Jesus answered, 'Peter, you do not understand the real reason I do this; if I do not wash your feet, then you cannot share my lot. '

'If that be so,' replied Peter, 'then stop not at washing my feet, but bathe the whole of me.'

Then, speaking in spiritual terms, Jesus said, 'When someone has bathed as you have, he is already clean and needs only to have the dust washed from his feet. This applies to all my followers.' Then recalling that one of them was to betray him that night, Jesus added, 'Well all except one of you.' Then, having completed washing the feet of all those present, Jesus put on his outer robe once more and sat down at the table.

Looking at those seated about him, Jesus said, 'I would ask you to consider what I have just done. You call me Master...Teacher...Lord, and this is as it should be since I am all these things to you. Yet as I, your Master, have been quite happy to wash your feet, likewise also should all of you be prepared to wash the feet of each other. I have set you an example; no servant is more important than his master, just as no messenger is more important than the man who sends him. Once you realize this truth, and behave accordingly, then will you find happiness in it.'

With great solemnity and some emotion in his voice, Jesus said, 'I was aware of what I was doing when I chose each of you (the apostles) I knew from the beginning that one of you seated at this table was to betray me, for my end has been predicted by the prophets; but woe to him who delivers me into the hands of them that seek to destroy me, for he will wish that he had never been born.'

Looking at each other in sad astonishment, his followers said 'Surely this cannot be? Who would do such a thing?' Then each of them began asking, 'Who is it? Is it me?' Jesus answered, 'It is him who dipped his bread into the dish with me.' Since one of them could recall who this had been, John, him who was deepest in the affections of Jesus, said, 'Please Master, tell us who it is.' Whereupon, picking up a piece of bread, Jesus said, 'It is he to whom I give this,' and after dipping the bread into a dish of herbs, Jesus handed it to Judas.

'Is it I, Teacher,?' Judas asked. Nodding confirmation, Jesus then said to Judas, 'Go quickly, and do what you have to do.'

Since Judas was the treasurer of the group, the full significance was not grasped at that precise moment, and the followers assumed, wrongly, that Jesus was sending him to purchase something needed for the Festival, Judas however, realizing that Jesus seen into the darkest recesses of his mind, immediately rose from the table and left the room.

With Judas gone, Jesus then addressed himself to the rest of his followers, saying, 'I have so brief a time left here with you. The time is very near for me to be glorified, and for me to glorify God. In honouring him, he will honour me. Where I go, you cannot for the moment follow, and I charge you all to love each other, even as I have loved you. For this love will set you apart as my followers from all other men.' Then, pausing for a moment and casting a glance slowly around the room, he said, 'You will all betray me tonight; it has been written, *I shall strike down the shepherd, and his sheep will scatter.* Regardless of this, when risen from the grave, I shall go on ahead of you to Galilee.'

'Everyone else may forsake you, but never I,' protested Peter.

'Peter,' said Jesus, 'Satan has desire to use you, but I have prayed that your faith will not run out, and when at last you are able to stand up to Satan and act without fear of him, then Peter shall you strengthen the others.'

'Tell us Master, where actually are you going?' asked Peter.

'Where I am going doesn't really matter,' answered Jesus, 'For the time being you cannot follow me, though you shall later.'

'Why can't I?' protested Peter, 'I am ready to die for you.'

Jesus answered, 'Peter, you say this here and now, but the truth is that before the cock crows the dawn you will have denied knowing me three times.'

'No Master! Not even if it means prison,' cried Peter, 'I will never let you down, and will die at your side if need be.'

Immediately all the other followers echoed Peter's words, but Jesus lifted his arm and quietened them, saying 'When I sent you out on journeys without money, spare clothing, or even an extra pair of sandals, did you ever lack for anything?'

'No,' they replied.

'Well now I am telling you that if you do have extra clothing, money, or sandals, take them with you this night. Likewise if you have a sword, take this also, for the Scripture reads, *he was classed as a criminal,* and all that has been predicted about me *will* happen.'

'We have two swords amongst us,' someone called.

'That is enough,' said Jesus. 'Do not despair when I have gone, and believe in me as you believe in God. I go to prepare places for you in my Father's kingdom, and when the time is right, then shall you all in your turn join me. You know where I am going, and you all know the way.'

'But we don't know where you are going,' protested Thomas, 'so how can we possibly know the way?'

'I myself am the way,' answered Jesus, 'I am truth; I am life; The only way to God is through me. If you have truly recognized me, then you would know who my Father is. However from now on you will know him because you have known me.'

'If you had allowed us to see the Father,' said Philip, 'then would we be convinced.'

'Is it possible Philip, that we have been together all this time, and you are still unaware of who I am?' replied Jesus. 'How can you say "Let us see the Father", when to see me is to see the Father? Do you still not realize that He and I are one? When I speak, it is the words of the Father you hear. If you find my oneness with him impossible to believe, then judge by the things you have seen me do in the past. The fact is that if you truly believe in me, not only will you be able to perform the works you have seen me do, but greater works still, because I shall be with the Father. Ask anything; ask on my authority and so that God may be honoured, and I will grant it.

'If you really love me, you will live by what I have taught you. I am going to ask the Father to give you someone in my place, someone to counsel, encourage, and be with you for ever. Who is this to be? The Spirit of truth. The world, because it does not have the ability to recognize or comprehend who he is, will not welcome him. You will know him, because he is in your hearts now, and will live in your hearts for ever. I shall not abandon you—I shall return in one form or another. Soon I shall be taken from the public gaze, but you shall see me, and my return from the grave will be my proof that all *do* and *will* live for ever (in a spirit body). Understand that my oneness with the Father is the same as my oneness with you. Prove your love to me by your obedience. Show your love for God and me, and I will return your love and reveal myself to you.'

'Master, you said you were going to reveal yourself to us, but not to the world,' said one of the disciples, 'would you explain this?'

'How much is revealed to you is dependent on your obedience to the Father. I have taught you a great many things in the time that I have been with you, but when I am gone then the Father will send someone else to counsel you—the one of whom I spoke a moment ago—the Holy Spirit. He will be your Teacher. He will remind you of what I taught.

'My legacy to you is peace, but my peace is a very different version of what the world calls peace. You must not fear, for as I said a moment ago, I may leave you (in materialistic form) but I shall return (in a spiritual form). If you really love me you will be happy that I go to rejoin the Father. He is greater than I. The reason I tell you this in advance is so that your faith shall not falter when these things begin to happen.

'My time with you is almost ended, for the unseen Ruler of the world draws near. It is not that he has authority over me, only that I am obedient to the Father, and thus show the world my love of him.

'Let me explain our relationship with an analogy. Think of me as an actual vine, and of yourselves as the branches, and of the Father as a gardener. If a branch fails to give fruit he cuts it away, but fruitful branches he prunes that they may give even greater yield, as you my followers have been pruned through my teachings. To remain fruitful it is necessary that you remain attached to me, and I to you, for just as in nature a branch cannot bear fruit unless it be attached to the vine. Apart from me you will produce nothing; in fact you will be thrown away, just as a broken branch is thrown away. Live each day attached to me, and my teachings will thrive in you. When you are fruitful you bring honour to the Father, and anything you ask may be granted. I love you in the same way that the Father loves me. Live always in my love. How?...By being obedient to my commandments, and the commandments of the Father. I tell you all this that you may give me good reason to rejoice, and that your happiness may be complete.

'What do I require of you? That you shall love each other as I have loved you—and who can love more than someone who is willing to die for his friends? You ARE my friends if you are willing to follow my teachings. Think of yourselves not as servants, for a servant does not share in the confidences of his master. That you are my friends I have proved by revealing all that the Father has revealed to me. You did not choose me, it was I who chose you and determined that you should be fruitful. The greatest commandment is, "Love each other".

'Do not however be surprised that when you offer love to your fellow men, they return your love with hatred—they hated me first. They would like you to be materialistic just as they, and because you refuse to be, they will hate you. I have already told you that the servant is no greater than his master, and because of this my persecutors shall also be your persecutors, just as those who were willing to follow me will also follow you. Some will despise and spit on you because of me, because in their ignorance they are not aware of who sent me here. It is because they HAVE heard of me, yet stop up their ears to what I say, that they become guilty and shall be left without any excuse to live in sin, since they choose this for themselves. Hating me, they are guilty of hating the Father. They stand condemned because they have seen and heard what I have done, such as no other man in history before me has done, yet still they continue to hate me and the Father. In fact it is the fulfilment of the old prophecy: *they hate me without cause.*

'At those times when the Holy Spirit shall come to you from the Father—he who is the very essence of truth and shall always be your counsellor and strength he will make revelations to you and it will be your work to pass these on to others.

'I tell you these things as a warning, for the time will come when so-called "religious" men will excommunicate you, indeed some will even try to kill you in the misguided belief that they are doing the will of God! Far from doing the will of God, they will only be revealing how little they truly understand me or the Father.'

Pausing for a moment, Jesus said, 'When I have departed, and the counsellor shall come to you, he shall make clear to the world what sin is, what goodness is, and what the judgment is all about. He will make it clear that the greatest sin is to reject me, and that goodness stems from the manner in which I depart to be for ever with the Father, and that judgment is brought by the sentencing of the invisible Ruler of this world and His invisible spirit-servants.

'A great deal has still to be revealed to you, but none of you are sufficiently suitable subjects to absorb the whole truth at this stage; it will however be given to you at a later date when you are visited by the Spirit of truth. it is he who will show you what lies ahead, and will be the Spirit Guide (instrument) through whom the Father and myself shall make our wishes known to you and all mankind.

'I must leave soon,' Jesus said, 'but will return a short time later.' Then, seeing how puzzled were the expressions of his followers, Jesus said, 'You clearly do not understand my meaning when I speak of leaving you, or of my return. The fact is you will shortly be mourning for me and shedding tears, though your tears of sorrow will very soon turn to tears of great joy—like a woman who in labour is in anguish, but whose anguish is quickly forgotten and replaced with joy and happiness when her baby is born. In the same way you will go through a time of sorrow, but this will in turn change to supreme happiness when you see me again, for you WILL see me again, I do assure you. When that moment comes you will not have any questions to ask, because suddenly all will be made clear to you; so much which your minds are not capable of grasping at this moment will become crystal-clear to you.

'Up to now, much of what I have said to you has been in figures of speech, but the time has now come to speak of the Father in straightforward language. When in your thoughts and prayers you speak to the Father in my name, there will be no need for me to intervene on your behalf. Understand that He Himself will love you, firstly because you love me, and secondly because you now accept that I came to earth at His bidding, and am returning to Him for the same reason.'

'Indeed we now understand much that has puzzled us to date,' said one of the disciples, 'and are all convinced that you are from God.'

'So you believe now, do you?' said Jesus, 'yet the time draws near when you will all be scattered, each fearing for his own safety, leaving me alone to face those seeking to destroy me. No, I should not say alone, for the Father will be with me. All I have told you has one purpose, and one purpose only—to bring peace. The world shall pass through times of testing, but have cheer, men of earth, for I have already conquered the world; use the knowledge I can and do impart to those who give their love and obedience to me, to conquer fear and adversity.'

Now Jesus turned his eyes towards heaven, and addressing himself to God said, 'Father, the hour is come. Honour me that I may honour you. You gave me authority over all mankind, authority to open the eyes of all men who seek the truth. I have honoured you by doing all that you gave me to do, and now, Father. I am ready to be restored to that state I had with you before the world began.

'These men you led to me. I have opened their eyes, and they have been obedient to me. They are now aware that everything I have comes from you, and that the words I utter are indeed yours, and that indeed I was sent here by you. I pray for these men—not the world—but these men who are my followers. They are yours, just as everything of mine is yours, as everything of yours is mine—and they have brought honour to me, to you. Now I am ready to leave this world and rejoin you, though they must remain here, I would ask you holy Father to sustain them, and give unto them that same oneness that exists between you and myself. Here on earth I have kept them in your name, kept all of them except that child of hell who was chosen that the Scriptures might be fulfilled. I have explained to these my followers what lies ahead of me, so that they may share in my happiness. I have given them your commands, and this had led to them becoming hated by this world because they are different...different from the world in the same way that I am. Father I ask now that you protect them from all evil. Purify them with the truth, the truth of your word. In the same way which you sent me into the world,

I send them out into the world also. I hereby consecrate myself for their sake so that they, too, may be consecrated by the truth.

'I pray, not only for these my followers, but also for all those men and women who will come after them and believe in me because of them. My prayer is that they may all become one with us, as we are one with them. You have honoured me, and I have passed that honour on to them, so that they may become one as are we—I with you, you with me—to prove to the world that I was sent by you, and that you love them as you love me. Dear Father, I desire these men to know how, out of your love for me, you honoured me before the earth was created. The world does not know you as I do oh righteous Father, but these my followers know I came from you. I have made you known to them, and will continue to do so, so that your love for me may be in their hearts even as I shall be always.'

Having thus prayed, Jesus remained in silent meditation a few moments longer, then opening his eyes he said to his followers, 'It is time for us to go.' Then, getting to their feet, they all joined in a hymn of praise, after which they quietly left the room and made their way to the dark streets outside.

# 34

## *The Master is arrested*

In the failing light, Jesus and his followers made their way to the Gardens of Kedron, also commonly known as the Gardens of Gethsemane, and as they entered these, Jesus, turning to his followers said, 'I wish to pray in private—wait here for me.' Then as an after-thought he said, 'Peter, James and John—come with me.'

They walked a short distance away and suddenly Jesus became convulsed with grief, much to the distress of the three apostles. 'Oh my soul!' he cried, 'The agony! I can hardly bear it! Stay here and keep a lookout while I go a little further on.' Then as they watched him walk a few steps away, he threw himself down onto a great slab of stone and cried out, 'Oh my Father, you who are able to do anything, please let me draw back from this agony if it be at all possible. But if this cannot be, then thy will be done, for thy wish is my command.'

As Jesus lay upon the stone in great agony of spirit, perspiration running down his face, the Holy Spirit came to him, calming his tortured mind and bringing him the peace and resolution he needed.

After a while Jesus rose to his feet, and seeing that the three apostles had fallen asleep, he went over to where they lay and gently nudging them said 'Could you not stay awake for even an hour to keep watch? I know the mortal body is a weak thing, but try to stay awake.' Then Jesus went back to pray yet again, returning a short time later looking very serene, calm and composed. Together with Peter, James and John they then rejoined the others.

He was conversing freely with them, speaking of the heavenly kingdom and his return to it, when in the thick darkness of the garden they saw lights approaching. All nature was silent and even the stars veiled their faces, refusing to look upon the impending deed of darkness. The lights of the flickering flambeaus showed a large band of armed men approached bearing swords, spears and bows—all these to capture but one man and a few unarmed followers! As they drew near it was seen that they were being guided by Judas.

Jesus seemed quite unmoved, merely telling his followers to remain calm and offer no resistance. Then, when the temple guards came up and surrounded him, Jesus asked, 'Whom do you seek?' They answered, ' Jesus of Nazareth,' and he replied, 'I am he.' Then an amazing thing happened. As if stricken, the whole band of armed soldiers fell flat on their faces to the ground—the rough soldiers of Rome, unaccustomed to bowing the knee and doing homage to a king—suddenly falling prostrate before him who they had come to arrest! But Judas the traitor stepped forward and kissed Jesus on the cheek. 'Do you betray me with a kiss then?' asked Jesus.

At length an officer ordered the guards to seize Jesus, but Peter, who was armed with a sword, boldly attacked them, severely wounding a servant of the high priest by cutting off his right ear. 'Stop, Peter!' cried Jesus, 'Put away your sword. Live by violence and you will die by violence. Do you not want me to obey God? You know that if I wish I could call down angels to rescue me, but that is not the Father's wish. The Scriptures must be fulfilled.' Then Jesus touched the bloody wound of the high priest's servant, and he was immediately healed. Oh Caiaphas, where was the sorcery in this? The later-life of the man who had been healed gave the answer, for he was later to become prominent as a spreader of the truth in Judaea. That passionate stroke of Peter's made numerous converts that night, more than had ever been made during all the missions of the Master.

As the soldiers bound the hands of Jesus and started to lead him away, his followers began to panic and fled in all directions. One of them (not an apostle), was seized by a soldier but so fiercely did he struggle that his robe came away in the hands of the soldier, and the young man fled quite naked into the engulfing darkness.

The temple guards marched Jesus to the house of Annas, father-in-law of the high priest, who then proceeded to interrogate him concerning his teachings.

Peter had followed the soldiers at a safe distance, and on reaching the house of Annas, he slipped into the courtyard of the building, where a large number of inquisitive people were beginning to gather. It was a cold night, and an officer of the guard and some household servants had built a fire in the centre of the enclosure. Peter had at first stood in the dark shadows of the surrounding buildings, but after a while he edged nearer to the fire that he might warm himself. As he did so, one of the housemaids recognized him and said, 'You are a follower of that man Jesus, aren't you?' Startled, but trying to remain calm, Peter answered, 'What are you talking about woman?—I don't even know the man.' Then, quickly but cautiously, he moved away from the light of the fire into the shadows once more, but once again he was recognized by a female servant, who immediately whispered to some men standing nearby, 'That man there, he is a follower of Jesus I have seen them together!'

'You ARE one of his followers aren't you?' called a man.

'No I am NOT!' protested Peter, 'I swear I'm not.'

Time passed, and just as Peter was confidently feeling safe again, yet another of Annas's servants came up to him and said, 'Didn't I see you in the Garden of Gethsemane earlier this evening with Jesus of Nazareth?'

'You most certainly did not!' said Peter, doing his best to sound indignant.

'But I did,' asserted the servant, 'You are one of his people— a Galilean , I would know that accent anywhere.'

Alarmed and in fear by now, Peter began to curse and swear, 'You are quite wrong, ' he shouted, 'I tell you I do not know the man!' Almost immediately , a rooster close by began to crow, and remembering how Jesus had earlier prophesied that he (Peter) would deny knowing his Master three times before the cock crowed, Peter broke down and cried bitterly.

Inside the house, Annas had been interrogating Jesus 'I have always spoken quite openly,' said Jesus, 'be it in temple, synagogue or market place. I have conducted nothing in secret. If you wish to know what I have preached, you have only to ask those who have listened to me.' Taking this to be impertinence, one of the soldiers struck Jesus in the face. 'How dare you talk to a priest like that,' he said.

'If I have answered wrongly, tell me how,' said Jesus, 'otherwise tell me why you struck me.' The soldier ignored him.

Annas now had the guards take Jesus, still bound, to the house of Caiaphas, where in the early hours of the morning the council was now assembling to hear potential witnesses, in the hope that someone could be found whose testimony would provide them with grounds on which to seek a death penalty for Jesus. They had found one man who was prepared to swear to hearing Jesus claiming that he would tear down the 'man-made temple' and build another ' quite untouched by human hands', but they were unable to find a second person who would substantiate this story. However, eventually two men were found whose stories did agree.

Rising from his great throne, Caiaphas charged Jesus: 'These men say you claim the power to destroy the temple and rebuild it again in only three days—what say you to this?' Jesus did not answer. So next Caiaphas asked, 'Are you the Christ?' Jesus replied, 'If I said yes you would not believe me, and were I to put questions to YOU, you would not answer.'

Furious at this evasion, Caiaphas angrily shouted, 'In the presence of the living God I demand you tell us if you ARE the Christ—God's son.'

'I am,' said Jesus simply, 'and you, Caiaphas, will yet see the son of man seated at God's right hand for yourself.'

Beside himself with rage, Caiaphas tore his robe ceremoniously to display ultimate disgust. 'Blasphemy!' he screamed, 'blasphemy!—You all heard him. We need no further witnesses, for he has condemned himself out of his own mouth.' Then he called to the council 'What is your verdict?'

'Guilty!' they cried 'He deserves to die.'

Immediately, the soldiers guarding Jesus began to slap him and spit in his face. Then one of the priests took a blindfold and, having covered Jesus's eyes, struck him. 'Come Messiah,' jeered the man, 'tell us who struck you?'

The religious leaders of the nation having condemned Jesus, Caiaphas order that he be taken to the king, Herod, and the soldiers dragged Jesus from the chamber, pummelling and punching him as they went.

At the palace he was brought into the presence of Herod, who was delighted to come face to face with the man he had heard so much about. Could he in truth perform the many miracles that had been attributed to him?—Herod was eager to find out. Putting questions to Jesus, he asked for some evidence of who he claimed he was, and asked him to give a demonstration of his powers, but Jesus would say and do nothing. In disappointed rage, Herod told the soldiers to take the prisoner back to Caiaphas.

# 35

## *Brought before Pilate*

It was now morning on the day of Preparation for the Passover, and Caiaphas had again called together all the chief priests, scribes, and members of the council to decide what steps should be taken in the execution of Jesus. When the meeting was at an end, they had Jesus brought before them again, and then marched to the Praetorium, to be convicted by the Roman governor of the state, Pontius Pilate.

Reaching the Praetorium, the priests and scribes would not enter the building because to enter the dwelling of a 'non-believer' would defile them, and they wished to eat the meal of the Passover later. Because of this, Pilate came to speak with them outside.

'With what crime do you charge this man?' asked Pilate. 'He had been corrupting the people, and has told them not to pay taxes to Caesar. In addition to this he also claims to be a king,' came the reply.

'Go judge this man by your own laws,' said Pilate.

'But we wish to sentence him to death, and we have no authority to do so,' they said.

Striding into the courthouse, Pilate told the guards to bring Jesus before him. 'Are you the king of the Jews?' he asked. 'Is that a personal question of your own, or did others suggest it?' said Jesus.

'I have no personal axe to grind,' Pilate said 'It makes no difference to me, I am not a Jew. You were brought here by your own countrymen—why? What is your real crime?'

'My kingdom is no earthly domain,' answered Jesus.

'So you are a king after all then?' said Pilate.

'If you say I am,' replied Jesus. 'That is why I was born, why I came to this world—to be the witness to truth, and those with truth in their hearts know this to be so.'

'What IS truth?' exclaimed Pilate, and realizing that Jesus's only crime was his belief, Pilate walked outside to the waiting crowd of priests and scribes, and said, 'I cannot find this man guilty of any crime.'

'But he is trying to stir up the people against the State,' they protested 'All over Judaea and Galilee he makes trouble with his teachings.'

Turning to Jesus, Pilate said, 'You hear their accusations?—What have you to say?' Jesus made no response, and Pilate was both intrigued and puzzled by the persistent silence of this man who would offer nothing in his own defence. The gentle dignity with which Jesus carried himself in front of this howling pack of wolves disturbed Pilate greatly, and when a moment later a servant arrived from his wife, pleading with him not to get involved in any judgment on Jesus because she had experienced a dream declaring him to be innocent, Pilate was even more concerned, for the Romans attached great importance to dreams. Therefore in an attempt to save Jesus Pilate said to the angry crowd before him, 'As you know, it is the custom for the governor to declare an amnesty each year during Passover, and to release to you any prisoner of the people's choosing...You brought Jesus to me and I cannot find him guilty of any crime, neither could Herod, for he sent him on to me I therefore propose that Jesus be flogged and then released.

At the mere mention of Jesus being released, the priests and their supporters went into a frenzy, shouting out 'Release Barabbas, not Jesus!' (Barabbas was a well known and popular criminal who had been sentenced for murder during a recent insurrection).

'Then what am I to do with Jesus?' said Pilate.

'Crucify him!' they cried.

'Why? For what crime? I found him guilty of nothing deserving such a penalty,' said Pilate.

'Crucify him! Crucify him!' the crowd roared all the louder.

Pilate was greatly disturbed that these people were so vindictive towards a man of obvious goodness and gentle ways, and decided he would have no part in their evil plans. Seeing that the crowd was near to riot, he called for a basin of water, and publicly as well as symbolically washed his hands in front of them, saying, 'I will accept no responsibility for the death of this innocent man.'

'His blood be on us and our children,' the crowd shouted (and this it most certainly has been, as the centuries that followed were to prove).

Pilate, now turning to his officers, ordered that Barabbas be released, and Jesus be flogged and crucified.

Having led Jesus away, the soldiers stripped him of his clothes and flogged him. Then, thinking to mock him and make sport, they threw a purple robe about his shoulders and twisting several branches from a thorn bush into the form of a crown, rammed this harshly down onto his head. One soldier then thrust a stick into his hand to resemble a sceptre and, kneeling in front of him, several of them began chanting, 'Hail, oh king of the Jews!' Other soldiers struck him about the face and body, and spat on him.

The flogging completed, Jesus was taken to Pilate once more, and leading Jesus out into the view of the angry crowd of Jews gathered there, Pilate cried, 'Here—once more I bring this man before you, and I wish it to be clearly understood, I find no wrong in him.' Pilate had hoped that the sight of the bruised and battered Jesus might now move the Jews to pity, but he was mistaken. 'Crucify him!' they shouted even louder.

'But he is an innocent man,' protested Pilate 'I find him guilty of nothing.'

'He has declared himself to be the son of God, and for that he must die,' they shouted. 'If you release him you are no friend of Caesar's,' cried one angry priest, 'for anyone who sets himself up as a king must be Caesar's rival.'

Feeling deeply troubled, Pilate returned to the courthouse, followed by Jesus and those who guarded him. Inside the building Pilate asked Jesus, 'Where are you REALLY from?' Jesus would not answer. 'So you refuse to speak?' said Pilate ' Don't you realize that I have the power to execute you or pardon you as I wish?'

'You would have no power over me at all, were it not given you from above,' came Jesus's response, 'that is why your guilt in this matter is less than those who handed me over to you.'

Perplexed, Pilate knew not what to do. His conscience told him that Jesus should be released, but he knew that if he gave the order to do so, the Jewish priests and the leaders of the people would complain to Rome, and his position as governor might be adversely affected. Finally, his mind made up, Pilate strode outside and, having taken his place on the seat of judgment, he had Jesus brought before him yet again. Then to the assembled people he called out, 'Behold, I present to you your king.'

'Crucify him! Crucify him!' they demanded.

'Crucify your king?' asked Pilate.

'We have no king but Caesar!' came their reply. Whereupon Pilate handed over Jesus to be crucified. The soldiers, having first removed his purple robe, now dressed him in his own clothes and marched him away.

When Judas saw that Jesus, his Master, had been condemned to die, he went first to the temple and threw his thirty pieces of silver on to the floor, then he went and hanged himself.

# 36

*The crucifixion and resurrection*

The heavy wooden cross having been lifted and placed on his shoulders by the soldiers, Jesus was led through the streets of Jerusalem to his place of execution. After a while, weak from the flogging he had sustained earlier in the day, he collapsed under the weight of the cross. As he struggled to his feet again, the soldiers commandeered a bystander, a man called Simon from Cyrene, to carry the cross for him the rest of the way.

Also condemned to die that day were two other men, both criminals, and they became part of the procession which wound its way through the narrow streets. Jerusalem was crowded at that time with people from all parts of Judaea, and when the Roman guards on their prancing horses appeared with Jesus in their midst, many of the people wept, and some of those who had clamoured for his crucifixion now shed tears as they looked upon him who quietly and without complaint went on to a cruel and shameful death. Among those who wailed were a group of women, and as Jesus passed he said to them, 'Do not spend your tears on me, save them for yourselves and your children. For in the days ahead a childless woman shall consider herself lucky. For the time shall come when they will wish they had never been born, for if men do this when the tree is green and fruitful, what will they do when it is barren?'

On reaching a hill outside the city known in Hebrew as 'the place of the skull', the soldiers stripped Jesus of his raiment. Then, offering him a drink—a drug mixed with wine—which he refused, they laid him upon the cross and drove nails through his hands and feet. Then having done the same with the two criminals, they raised the crosses on top of the hill, and there between the two criminals hung the Prince of Glory, in agony and shame, amid a crowd of mocking, heartless Jews and rough

Roman soldiers. Yet even then there came forth from Jesus no sound of complaint, instead he only said, 'Father forgive them, for they known not what they do.'

On the cross over the head of Jesus, the Romans by command of Pilate, had placed an inscription in three languages (Hebrew, Latin and Greek). Evidently to spite the Jews, it read, *Jesus of Nazareth, the king of Jews,* and since this was clearly visible from the road leading to Jerusalem, the chief priests objected to it. They went to Pilate requesting that the wording be changed, 'king of the Jews, indeed!' they protested. But Pilate was adamant, 'Not a single word shall be changed,' he said, and the priests went away furious.

Under the cross the soldiers sat waiting for Jesus to die. Ripping up his clothing they began drawing lots for the best pieces. Picking up his robe it was noticed that it had been woven without a seam, and one of them said, 'It is a pity to tear this—Let us draw lots for the complete garment.' Thus unwittingly was fulfilled that scripture saying, THEY DIVIDED MY CLOTHES AMONG THEM AND CAST LOTS FOR MY ROBE.

While Jesus endured excruciating pain, the mocking taunts of the spiteful Jews continued: 'This is the man who had the power to pull down the temple and rebuild it again in only three days,' they jeered.

'Son of God!' shouted one man, 'Let us see you prove who you are by coming from that cross.' Another remarked, 'The great saviour of others cannot even save himself!'

'He claimed to be the son of God,' said a priest, 'Let us see if his Father will save him.'

Even one of the crucified criminals joined in, saying, 'If you are the Christ, don't just save yourself, but save us too while you are at it!' The second criminal, however, rebuked him saying, 'Don't you even know what it is to fear God? All three of us are dying; you and I deserved our punishment, but what has this man Jesus done? He is not a criminal.' Then, turning to face Jesus as best he could, he said, 'When you reach your kingdom, spare a thought for me.'

'Before this day is ended, you shall rest in the shade of green trees, and be refreshed with cool, clear water,' said Jesus.

Among those who continued to remain at the foot of the cross were a group of Jesus's followers, and although some of even the eleven apostles had deserted him, not one of the women who had so devotedly followed him was absent, and what bitter sorrow it was for them to see their beloved Master crucified in pain and in shame. They had witnessed his child-like submission and heard his words of love and deep compassion—his prayer for his murderers.

Among the women at the foot of the cross were his mother, her sister, and Mary Magdalene. Jesus, seeing his beloved disciple John standing among them, said to his mother, ' Look, there is your son.' Then to John he said, And there, my beloved friend, is your mother.' From that day on, Mary was to live in the home of John and under his care.

At noon Jesus had then been hanging on the cross for three hours, it grew strangely dark and remained so until three in the afternoon. Then suddenly, Jesus shouted 'My God! My God! Why hast thou forsaken me?'

'Listen,' said an onlooker 'he is calling to Elijah.' ' Well let us see if Elijah helps him!' another jeered.

Jesus, now knowing that his task was completed and that all the prophecies concerning himself had been fulfilled, let out one final groan of anguish, crying out, 'Father, I commit my spirit to Thy hands,' then his head fell forward, he gasped, 'It is finished,' and died.

At the moment he died, the curtain at the entrance to the holy of Holies in the temple, tore from top to bottom. The darkness increased, vivid flashes of lightning forked across the sky in every direction and thunder rolled most fearfully. Then the earth began to shake beneath their feet, and terror was pictured on the faces of everyone. While large crowds of Jews slunk away in consternation towards Jerusalem, Roman soldiers who were never afraid of ten times their number in battle, crouched as if expecting the heavens to fall on them, and more educated Romans remarked, 'Surely this man is the son of a Divine being.'

During the great darkness, it was said that the spirits of man who had long passed away returned to Jerusalem and were seen by many. There were some so silly as to say that they had resumed their old bodies which had lain for ages in the grave, but if they appeared at all it can only have been in bodies materialized for the occasion.

As night drew on, some of Jesus's followers still knelt at the foot of the cross, and they were thus kneeling when the soldiers came to break the legs of the crucified before the Jewish sabbath began. The two malefactors, still alive, were quickly put out of their agonies by the soldiers. When they saw that Jesus was already dead and that there was no necessity to break his legs, one of the soldiers raising his spear, thrust it into Jesus's side, and blood and water poured forth.

Earlier that evening, Joseph of Arimathaea—he who had so boldly defended Jesus in that vile council which Caiaphas had called together—went to Pilate and got permission to remove the body of Jesus to a tomb he had prepared for it.

Joseph and Nicodemus, another member of the council who had spoken out in defence of Jesus, had gone to Golgotha, taken down the body and wrapped it in a winding-cloth, together with crushed myrrh and aloes as was the custom, and then transported it to the tomb hewn from rock in a garden nearby. Having placed the body in the tomb, they then rolled a huge stone over the entrance and returned to their homes.

That evening a large number of Jesus's followers had met together at the house of one of their group, and it can be imagined how heavy of heart they must have felt. But it was a night of prayer, and as the sabbath came on they felt that Jesus was there in spirit at least. When next morning they discovered that Joseph of Arimathaea had taken possession of their Master's body, great was their joy, though this could not banish the thought that he who had loved them so was now taken from their mortal sight. It was while they were in this condition that the venerable Issha, the old Egyptian priest who had been the tutor of Jesus during his boyhood, appeared to Hermes, one of the followers (he who had been a boyhood friend of Jesus). Issha said they should not be disquieted, for Jesus would soon be with them again, and that an angelic Host would watch over them until Jesus returned to give them the power which he had promised.

All Jerusalem was now in commotion because of what had taken place the day before. The priests, pondering on the few words that had fallen from the lips of Jesus regarding his rising again, set a guard of soldiers to watch the tomb where Joseph had laid the body, lest, as they said, the followers of Jesus should attempt to steal it away and claim that he had risen again. Poor men! They knew not (but they might have known from their own sacred writings) that all the legions of Rome could not keep him entombed. No, had he been built up in a solid pyramid of stone, nothing could have prevent the son of the highest returning to his sorrowing brethren.

And when the sabbath was past, and the morning light came on, did the Great Deliverer burst out upon the soldiers in the greatness of his power? No, he quietly passed through the doorway, and in the sight of the trembling guards, who bowed before him, he left them to watch an empty tomb. The soldiers, on recovering from their astonishment at that which they had seen, went and reported to the priests all that had taken place. And what did these evil-hearted men do? It was said they attempted to bribe the poor soldiers into admitting that while they slept the body of Jesus had been taken away by his followers. 'Only do this, and we will make it right with your commander,' they had said, for well the priests knew that it was death by Roman law for a soldier to sleep while on guard.

Such were the men who crucified Jesus—chief priests in the temple of God! Dastards! To attempt poor soldiers with a bribe. They tried to hide the truth, but they were defeated. They had but to look at the rent veil of their temple to see heaven's condemnation of their accursed deed. Had every such a thing happened before? It was no earthly power which did that. The fire of heaven had cleft it in twain, and the word went forth—Away with all these mummeries! The day of symbols is past. Not now by these need man approach his Maker. Man's *heart* is the true temple of God. Conscience will guide man, the Lesser Intelligence, to serve God the Great Intelligence. And Jesus the Light of the world, will destroy the corrupt systems of men.

Early on the Sunday morning, just before dawn, Mary Magdalene, Mary the mother of James, and Salome set out for the tomb, taking with them spices with which they intended to embalm the body of Jesus, As they approached the tomb, they were discussing how best they might move the heavy stone from the entrance, when to their utter amazement they saw that the entrance to the tomb was already open. Going into it, they found no body, but where Jesus had lain there remained now only the winding-cloth he had been wrapped in. The next moment, two spirit messengers materialized before them, dazzling white in appearance. Terrified, the women hid their eyes, but in a gentle voice of the spirits said, 'Do not be afraid. The Master has risen, and he bids you tell all his followers that he will meet with them in Galilee, just as he said he would. Go now, hurry and tell all the followers.'

Trembling with a mixture of astonishment and happiness, the women hurried from the tomb and made their way to the house where the followers were gathered. Here Mary Magdalene related to the group what they had seen and been told. A few voiced the opinion that the grief of the women was playing tricks with their imagination, and others said it was too incredible to be true, however Peter and John without hesitation ran from the house and headed for the tomb as fast as their legs could carry them.

John was the first to arrive and, pausing to get his breath back, he leaned on the side of the entrance and peered in. Such enough they lay the linen bandages on the ground, but he felt too nervous to go in.

Moments later Peter came up and, without hesitation, went straight into the tomb. John followed behind. Certainly the body of Jesus was gone, but what amazed Peter and John most was the fact that the linen bandages had *not been unwrapped...*it was though the body must have completely exhaled itself (dematerialised) without disturbing either the wrappings, or the fastenings. Recalling how years earlier they had been privileged witnesses on Mount Hermon, when both Moses and Elijah had materialized to speak with Jesus, it suddenly dawned on them exactly how Jesus had 'Risen'. Of course he was not 'dead'—he had simply passed into another phase of existence, as Moses and Elijah had, and everyone else who had 'died'. At last they fully understood what Jesus had meant when he had implied that there was no such thing as 'death'. It also made them understand that if it were possible to go from one phase of existence to another, from material to spirit, then it was equally possible for spirit to return to a material existence (materialise) if so desired. Now Peter and John *knew* they would indeed see their beloved Master again, and this above all else with the understanding Jesus had tried to impart to his followers—understand that much, and other knowledge would follow more easily.

Full of joy now, Peter and John returned to tell the other followers the good news.

In the meantime Mary Magdalene, puzzled by the disappearance of Jesus's body, had returned crying to the tomb once more. Peering through the entrance into the dark interior, the two bright spirits she had seen earlier, suddenly reappeared. 'Why do you cry, woman?' asked one. 'Because my Lord's body has gone—and I know not where,' sobbed Mary. Then as quickly as the spirits had appeared, so they were gone again. But then, standing in the dark shadows of the tomb's interior, Mary noticed another figure standing. Thinking it might be the gardener—it was really too dark to see properly—Mary begged, 'Sir' if you know the whereabouts of my Lord's body, please tell me.' He spoke but one word: 'Mary,' but it was enough for her to recognize his voice. 'Master!' cried the elated woman, and she rushed forward to embrace him. However, in the dim light and in her emotional state, Mary did not realise that the transition from his material body to the spiritual body (and vice versa) were not yet complete, and so quickly Jesus had to curb her enthusiasm: 'Do not cling to me, Mary,' said Jesus, 'I am not yet fully returned to my Father. Go tell my disciples that I am on the way to joining my Father and my God, your Father and God.'

In a state of great excitement, Mary now rushed off to the house where the disciples were staying, 'I have seen the Lord,' she cried, 'and he has given me a message for you.'

Not far away that same day, two disciples (Cleopas and another) were leaving Jerusalem to return to their home in the village of Emmaus, some seven miles away. As they walked and discussed the events of the last few days, they were joined by a stranger who asked if he might walk along with them for company. (The 'stranger' was in fact Jesus materialised in a form not known to them). 'What were you discussing?' the stranger asked. 'Jesus of Nazareth,' came the reply. 'Why? What has happened?' the stranger asked. Staring at him in amazement, the disciples exclaimed, 'Do you mean to say you do not known what has been happening in Jerusalem these past few days? You must be the only visitor to the city who doesn't!' Then Cleopas explained: 'Jesus was a prophet who did the most astonishing things, and we—his disciples—were all hoping that he would free Israel from these hated Romans. But the chief priests had him arrested and turned over to the Romans to be crucified. That was three days ago, and yet yesterday some women from our group came to us claiming that they had been to the tomb of Jesus, only to find that his body had vanished! They also claimed that two angels had appeared, telling them that Jesus was alive and we would see him again. Some of our group then went at once to the tomb to verify the women's story—the body of Jesus had certainly vanished.'

'Men are so reluctant to accept the predictions of the prophets,' said the stranger. 'As the followers of Jesus, surely you must have realised that before he could be glorified, the

Messiah had first to endure some kind of suffering?' The stranger then began quoting Moses in the various scriptures, as well as others who had all given prophecies relating to Jesus.

Since by the time they reached Emmaus it had grown late, the two disciples suggested to the stranger that he should spend the night with them, and continue on his journey the following day. The stranger accepted, and they invited him to take a meal with them. At the commencement of the meal, the stranger picked up a piece of bread, and having said thanks to God for it, he broke it into pieces and gave some to each of them. Suddenly they realised his true identity, but in that same instant he began to dematerialise right before their eyes, and a moment later he was gone.

For several minutes the disciples looked at each other in astonishment, then one said to the other, 'Now we know why his explanation of the various scriptures warmed our hearts so.' They were also aware that by giving them this practical demonstration of dematerialisation, far more was achieved in explaining his disappearance from the tomb than a thousand spoken words could have done, and so anxious were they to tell the other disciples what had taken place that they left for Jerusalem immediately, arriving that same night.

Going straight to the house occupied by the apostles and other followers of Jesus, they hurried in to relate their wonderful news, but before they could open their mouths to speak, they were greeted by excited cries of, 'He is risen—Jesus has risen from the grave! He really has, Peter has seen him!'

As the followers talked excitedly about these recent developments, the spirit of the venerable Issha suddenly appeared in the room and everyone fell silent. Saying nothing, but raising his arms slowly, Issha then disappeared and almost immediately before the eyes of the wondering brethren there stood Jesus in bodily form. He stretched out his hands towards them and they were able to see the wounds the nails had made. Then he spoke, saying, 'I have been away and have seen my kingdom, and now I will be with you for a short time before I finally depart.' Some of the brethren thought it a vision, but others knew it was reality and that this was the same body they had so often looked upon before the crucifixion; yet there was some difference, not easily described. However, when Jesus grasped the hands of the followers, the feeling was the same as when they grasped the hands of each other. It was noted that he appeared sadder now, though in fact he had rarely smiled in the past. But now, he spoke with solemnity. He alluded to the opposition that would be made to the work of the followers, but told them not to be afraid, for he would ever be with them, that when the persecution set in against them because of the truth, they were to watch lest they should be tempted to fall away. 'Be ever bold and faithful in the work which I have given to you to do; never withhold your hands from the great work. A structure (church) will be raised, but as time goes on my doctrine will be trampled underfoot by men professing to be my true followers, but they will be hypocritical worshippers, wearing a clock of truth to cover their iniquity.' Then, just as suddenly as he had made his appearance before them, Jesus was gone.

One apostle, Thomas, had been absent from the house when Jesus had materialised, and when he later returned and was told all that had taken place, he found it impossible to believe: 'Not until I have seen the wounds in his hands for myself, and touched them, and seen the wound in his side will I believe it is truly him,' said Thomas.

It was some eight days later before Jesus made another appearance to all the brethren at the house, and this time Thomas was present too. 'Peace be unto all of you,' said Jesus, the he beckoned to Thomas saying, 'Thomas, come here,' and stretching his hands towards the disciple he said, 'Look upon my hands and touch my wounds.' Then drawing aside his robe, Jesus said, 'See too the wound in my side, and do not doubt.'

Satisfied now, Thomas exclaimed, 'My Lord and my God.'

However, Jesus rebuked him, saying, 'You believe only because you see. Happy are they who trust without proof.'

Again and again Jesus was to meet with his followers and speak of the necessity of prayer and watchfulness on their part, in view of the mission they were undertaking. These interviews with their beloved Master were held in various places, when they came together during the next few weeks, but none of them knew where he went to when he left them. He was seen by the brethren who were fishermen, walking on the shore at Galilee, by others on the Mount of Olives, while Hermes and others had seen him surrounded by the heavenly Host. Indeed, it might well be said that he met with the brethren by day, and with the angels by night. Hermes had seen some of these holy Ones in their mortal form in days gone by (Issha and Hafed for example), but in company with Jesus they appeared in spirit with a brightness beyond that of the sun at noonday.

As the day drew near when Jesus should leave them, he gave each one directions about the work to be undertaken. Although the Jews had crucified him, the brethren were not, he said, to throw such a charge in their faces, neither must the followers refuse the deal with them; on the contrary, they were to hold forth his truth to the people of Jerusalem, and if they as his followers were reviled because of their faith in him, then they were to submit, answering them not.

By day the followers went out into countryside with Jesus and, just as in the days prior to his crucifixion, the country people drew near to him, and he put forth his power, as he had done before, healing those among them who were sick.

At length they came to the spot where Jesus was to be taken from them, high on a mountain in Galilee. Here all the brethren gathered about him, while he prayed for them. Then in loud clear tones he said, 'With all the authority of the heavens and earth invested in me, I now command that each of you shall go out to all the surrounding nations, indeed to every corner of the world, spreading everywhere the good news of the kingdom. Baptize them in the name of the Father, the Son, and the Holy Spirit, and teach them to be obedient to every command I have given you. And remember, I shall be with you always.' Then, just as Jesus was in the act of blessing the brethren, he was gradually lifted up before their eyes. Gazing longingly upwards, they beheld a host of bright beings overshadowing them, and as Jesus and the whole host around him slowly rose, so all was dissolved into a great luminous cloud.

They saw no more of Jesus in the body after that, but they knew they would meet him in the heavens into which he had gone, and that although no longer with them in the body, he would be with them in the spirit to direct and guide them. With Jesus gone, the followers returned to Jerusalem as he had bidden, to wait on his promise—the fullness of spirit.

# 37

## *Persecution: Rome takes the reins*

The chief priests of Jerusalem thought they had forever destroyed Jesus and his teachings. What had they to fear from a dead man and a group of leaderless followers? Dead he most certainly was not, and neither was the truth they sought to destroy.

Cautiously biding their time, the brethren waited for the fulfilment of the promise, though there were some among them who did not even then comprehend Jesus's real meaning, thinking he would yet appear as the saviour of the nation from bondage. But there were others who knew better, and knew that his appearance would be spiritual; that he referred to the gift of spirit which he would bestow on them, so that they might be fully prepared to go out into the world and proclaim the truths he had taught them. This stronger element it was that endeavoured to keep up the heart of their weaker brethren in their daily meetings for prayer, and they ceased not in their supplications to the Most High that He would send forth His holy Ones to guard them from their enemies, who like lions lay ever ready to spring on them.

At length the day came. They were all assembled in the usual place, engaged in prayer, when the walls of the house were terribly shaken, as if by an earthquake, while lights of the blueish-white colour blazed above their heads, and beyond these strange lights they saw the Prince, their Master, in glory, surrounded by bright hosts of spirits.

While they gazed in wonder and amazement, the bright lights that had been flickering above, fell on their heads, and then it was that they felt the promise had been fulfilled—that they had received the power from the highest to fit them for their work. Thus were they equipped by their beloved Master, ready to do battle for him with the sword of the spirit.

It was one of the Hebrew festivals, when thousands were gathered together in Jerusalem from the surrounding nations, that the brethren went out and proclaimed the truth about Jesus to crowds of people in all different languages.

The effect on the minds of many was deep and lasting, and productive of much good, for these strangers from other lands, on returning to their homes, carried the truth with them, and thus became the pioneers of those brethren who were to follow them. And it was not long before they were followed, for from that day, when so many were drawn to listen to the brethren, persecution set in. Some of the followers were imprisoned—though their prison-doors were thrown open by unseen hands. The Jewish rulers were confounded, and knew not what to do so as to keep the common people in ignorance of such wonderful works. They were afraid that the populace would rise in rebellion against the Roman government, and thus bring down the heavy hand of Rome on the heads of the nation. The result was that many of the brethren were compelled to flee from Jerusalem.

The chosen apostles and others who remained proposed to form a council for the management of the work. Hermes and others felt bound to oppose this, since they felt it interfered with the liberty of individuals, and suggested that they should go out, two or three together, as the Spirit had directed, uncontrolled by the rule of a council who might seek to exercise lordship over brethren who were called to labour in distant countries. There should be but one Master, Hermes maintained, and each and all should be guided by His spirit what to do, and how to do it. But his counsel was rejected, and since the greater number were against him, he was forced to abide by their decision. However Hermes said that if he saw the spirit of lordship raising its head, then he would have nothing more to do with them, but would go out to the world and work freely in the cause of Jesus, his only Master. Certain rules for the ongoing work in Jerusalem were adopted. In Jerusalem they had all things in common—that is, rich and poor fared alike, all were on the level of brotherhood, and all were glad to do the Master's work.

The council was composed principally of the Hebrew disciples, with just a few from other countries. There were some dark-skinned sons of Africa, sleek-haired natives of India, and even some from islands in the far west called Britons; these were men who having first joined the Roman army in their own land, had come to serve in Judaea, then deserted from the army to become followers of Jesus. In such a mixed assembly it would have been strange had nothing occurred to disturb them.

The Hebrews, being the greatest in number, would have their own way, the impetuous Peter contending strongly for the observance by the brethren of certain Jewish rites and ceremonies. Violent discussions, in which some hot words were uttered, almost led to blows, for a number of the brethren who were foreigners and had drunk in the Master's doctrines were determined to crush this attempt of the Jewish brethren to bring all the rest of them under the yoke of Judaism. They maintained that such national distinctions should be cast aside, as they were opposed to the doctrines proclaimed by Jesus himself, which were not for the Jews only, but for the whole of mankind. However the council, as constituted, had but a short time to exist, for during the heat of the persecutions it was broken up and all were compelled to flee to various countries. Thus were the Master's doctrines and teaching spread far and wide to the ends of the then known world, although persecution was to take place almost everywhere they went, and thousands were to die for their faith before mighty Rome eventually adopted Christianity herself as the State Religion.

At first Christians everywhere must have rejoiced that their faith had overcome and conquered even Rome, but all too soon the newly established 'Church of Rome' was to destroy real Christianity far more effectively than ever three hundred years of persecution had done. The Ministry of the Spirit (the Spirit 'gifts'), which had formed the very essence of Christ's teachings, was now quickly outlawed and all spirit healers and mediums banished, and a very materially-minded Ministry of Office took control with all the accompanying lower ideals and practices. Worse still, the new church was to ascribe all the 'miracles' of Jesus to his Godhead, thereby completely divorcing him from the rest of humanity.

Centuries later, the Church of Rome would have fragments break from it to form independent churches of their own, though these too would continue to suppress the psychic truths which Jesus and his true followers had given the world, and thousands more would perish as heretics in defence of them. Only in the last few decades has this persecution halted to any degree, and now in the twentieth century has come the time for the world to realise that until Psychic Science is restored to its rightful place in the fabric of all Christian churches, then much of the Gospel will forever remain utterly incomprehensible to the vast majority of modern and reasoning people.

Love, peace, and harmony are surely things this world is desperately in need of, and only the truth can give it.